PILLOW PEOPLE

$5.95
$6.95
in Canada

Needlepoint
Designs for 40 Unusual
Doll Pillows

Bill Bragdon and Jeanne Harrison

PILLOW PEOPLE

PILLOW PEOPLE

Needlepoint Designs for 40 Unusual Doll Pillows

Bill Bragdon and Jeanne Harrison

HAWTHORN BOOKS, INC.
Publishers / New York

PILLOW PEOPLE

Copyright © 1976 by Bill Bragdon and Jeanne Harrison. Copyright under International and Pan-American Copyright Conventions. All rights reserved, including the right to reproduce this book or portions thereof in any form, except for the inclusion of brief quotations in a review. All inquiries should be addressed to Hawthorn Books, Inc., 260 Madison Avenue, New York, New York 10016. This book was manufactured in the United States of America and published simultaneously in Canada by Prentice-Hall of Canada, Limited, 1870 Birchmount Road, Scarborough, Ontario.

Library of Congress Catalog Card Number: 75-28697
ISBN: 0-8015-5875-1
1 2 3 4 5 6 7 8 9 10

To
Aunt Vi
Kurt
Dick and Jan
Annie

Contents

Acknowledgments

We would like to thank the following friends for their patience and cooperation during the preparation of *Pillow People*: Joan Barrow, Cara Burnham, Sanny Burnham, Sandra Choron, Anne Foster, Patsy Knack, Amy Lassen, Liza Leeds, Lydia Leeds, Jan Miner, Fran Nusbaum, Sharon Pransky, Ina Pursell, Teri Ralston, Kit Riley, and Cathy Van Rynn.

PILLOW PEOPLE

Introduction

If you are an avid needlepoint fan or if you are just a beginner, sooner or later you will develop a craving for something different to stitch up. It happened to us about two years ago. Until then we had been happily making the usual floral designs, the landscapes, the intriguing geometric patterns, and just about every walking and flying animal around.

Next came Bargello and the wonderful world of the Flame stitch, the Scallop, the Double Weave, the Algerian Eye, and so forth. Soon our houses and our friends' houses were overflowing with these stunning designs. Bargello is beautiful, but we found it can be deadly dull with the endless repetition of the same stitch. Besides, Bargello designs work much faster than the conventional design, because the stitch covers more area in less time than the standard diagonal stitch. We soon learned that Bargello may be fun and fast, but it can also be expensive. The quicker you finish one pillow, the sooner you start another. This can cost a lot of money!

Sometime during the last days of our Bargello mania while we were looking for something new to needlepoint, the first doll was born. Neither of us can really recall how we happened upon the idea of making needlepoint dolls, except that we were desperate and the doll design seemed to spark a new enthusiasm in both of us.

Looking back on the first few dolls we completed, they now seem rather crude and simple in design because we were experimenting with the type of doll we wanted to create. The earliest ones were always little ladies holding flowers: a nice design but not very creative and not unique. Slowly, though, our dolls began to take on personality as we began to expand our ideas and think of unusual designs. This is how the Pillow People came about; not all at once, but slowly.

About this time something else happened. Our friends started asking us for them. We began to realize that these funny little dolls made fantastic presents and that maybe we had hit upon a really new idea in needlepoint. Everyone who received a doll seemed so taken when they saw it for the first time. As a matter of fact, when we began assembling all the dolls for this book, we had to promise each friend and relative that each doll would be returned as soon as possible. Each doll had become a part of the family.

We also discovered something else about our new little people. You can make them and their clothing any color. Actually what this really means is that the dolls are an excellent way of using all those bits and pieces of leftover yarn you didn't have the faintest idea what to do with. We learned to use them for eye-liners, freckles, lips, rings, and so on. Any little area on the doll becomes the perfect place to use that one strand of puce you've had for years.

We quickly grew to love designing and making our dolls because they are different from any other kind of needlepoint. We don't want you to get the impression that we are crazy, but the kicks we get working on these dolls seem to stem from the fact that they do have personalities that develop as the design progresses. There have been many times when one of us would break up with laughter after finishing the nose or the mouth or the expression in the eyes. And what's more, you can change a doll's attitude or personality simply by altering the line of a stitch. It's really up to you to decide how closely you follow the designs in this book.

The important thing to remember is that needlepoint should be not only a relaxing hobby but self-satisfying and, most importantly, FUN. If you care to improvise on the design and make some changes, be our guest. Your alterations will personalize the design and make it all yours. But if you choose to go along with our designs, you still have the freedom to try different stitches and colors within the clothing, flowers, and shoes.

Before going on to the nuts and bolts of this book, we want to leave you with this thought: for the past two years we have had a ball designing and making the Pillow People dolls you are about to see. Now it is your turn to meet the little people and transform them into pillows for yourself or your friends. We just hope that they bring you as much enjoyment and pleasure as they have brought us.

1

How to Needlepoint

If you are just beginning the hobby of needlepoint, this chapter is meant for you. On the other hand, if you have been at it a long time, move on to the next chapter because you know everything we are about to explain—except, maybe, the Hair stitch found at the end of this chapter.

The starting point in any discussion about needlepoint should be the canvas with which you will be working. There are two types of canvas available in most stores: "mono" and "Penelope." This first

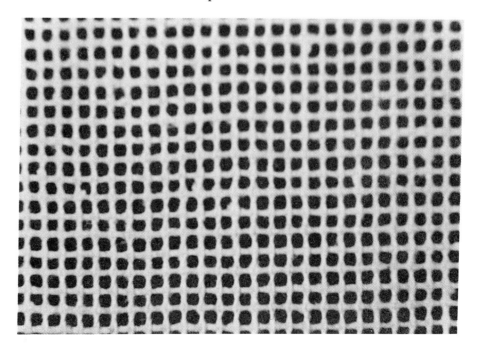

is a woven mesh of single, vertical, and horizontal threads. In our experience the mono canvas seems to be the most popular type, because it is easy to see and, therefore, easier to count the strands. The more complex Penelope canvas is made up of pairs of vertical and horizontal strands. This pattern allows you to stitch through the larger holes of the vertical pairs or work through the half-size holes of the individual paired strands for greater detail work. If the Penelope canvas sounds too complicated for you right now, don't worry because our designs are based on the mono.

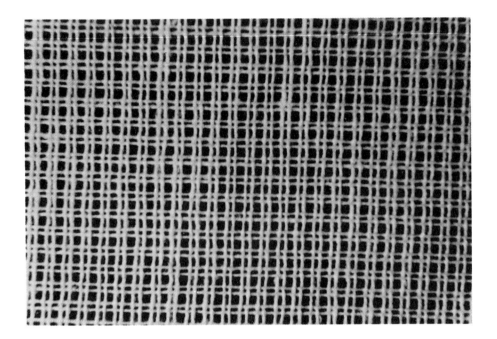

Whether mono or Penelope, needlepoint canvas may be purchased in varying sizes or gauges. To determine a canvas gauge all you have to do is count the number of vertical strands per inch. For example, a 14-gauge or "point" canvas has fourteen strands per inch, which allows for the same number of stitches per inch. If you want to work in greater detail, you would, of course, choose a high-count canvas because there are more stitches allowed per square inch. For the purposes of this book, we have based all the designs on ten strands per inch. This gauge is easy and quick to work and gives enough detail to bring out the personality in each doll.

We want to offer two helpful suggestions concerning the care of your canvas. When cutting the canvas, always make sure that you allow for a two- or three-inch border around the outside of the design. This area will not be stitched but is extremely important for blocking your piece. We will explain this blocking process in greater

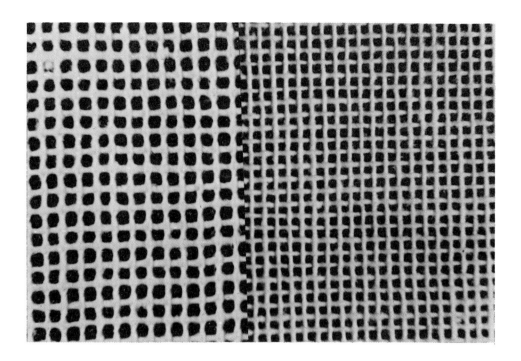

detail later on. Second, before working on any project, always secure the edges of your canvas. Some people suggest that you machine-stitch around the border, but that is too much work for us. A simpler solution is to buy masking tape. Using half the width of the tape, secure one side of the canvas. Then turn the canvas over and fold down the other half of the tape and secure it to the strands. In other words, you actually frame the border in tape, which prevents the canvas from unraveling during your work.

When choosing your yarn, we recommend that you stick with the Persian yarns found in all needlepoint stores. These yarns have been developed especially for needlepoint work. They are colorfast and woven from long fibers so they will last a long time and not fray. These yarns are usually made up of three strands, which can be easily pulled apart to mix colors for shading effects. For our purposes this 3-ply yarn is perfect for completely covering the 10-gauge canvas.

The only possible reason we can think of for passing by Persian yarns and heading for the five-and- ten-cent-store knitting wools is cost. Persian yarns are usually sold by weight and may range from a little over $1.00 to almost $2.00 per ounce depending on the store you select. On the other hand, a whole skein of knitting wool may cost the same price. But remember, this wool is woven from shorter fibers and tends to fray easily. Some of these wools tend to be elastic, which will pull your canvas out of shape. Also, the colors are not as vibrant or varied as the Persian yarns. The knitting wools should be used only when you need a certain effect that cannot be realized with the Persian. For example, one of our dolls, Elegant Edythe, is wearing a fox fur. In this case we used an angora wool for the furry effect.

The Basic Stitches

Bookstores are full of needlepoint books that explain the many, many different stitches that can be worked on the canvas. Most of these stitches are very exotic and produce fantastic patterns and gorgious designs. Any one of these or any combination could add new dimensions to our doll designs. As we mentioned earlier, we encourage you to improvise.

All of our designs have been created using only four different stitches: the Continental or Basketweave, the Brick stitch, the Florentine (Zigzag), and Turkey Tufting (the Hair stitch). If you can master these simple stitches, you will have absolutely no trouble with the Pillow People.

Before explaining these basic stitches, we would like to say a word about neatness. The final look of any needlepoint project depends to a great extent on just how neat you are when stitching. A cardinal rule for needlepointers is to keep the back of a canvas free from loose ends. Remember, when beginning a project, never knot the yarn. Instead, leave about one inch in the back and then catch that loose end in the first five or six stitches. From that time on when beginning a new piece of yarn, just slide your needle through a few of the back stitches to hold the yarn. And, please, always use scissors to cut off those little loose ends. If you forget to do this, you will soon learn that they have a nasty way of suddenly slipping through the stitched canvas and making a mess of your work.

The Continental Stitch

Most of the people we know seem to work with the Continental stitch. When asked why, they usually explain that this was the first stitch they learned, and they just haven't got around to learning anything new. The only reason we can find for the Continental's popularity is its simplicity. The stitch forms a diagonal from the lower left to the upper right and covers the intersection of one vertical and one horizontal strand. The stitch is always worked

	18	16	14	12	10	8	6	4	2
17	15	13	11	9	7	5	3	1	
	19	21	23	25					
20	22	24	26			15	2		
					16	1			
					13	4			
					14	3			
					11	6			
					12	5			
					6	8			
					10	7			

from right to left. When one row is completed, the canvas is turned upside down and worked back, right to left again. The diagram pictures the Continental stitch.

Starting at the back of the canvas, bring the needle out through 1 and in through 2; then out 3 and in 4, and so on. Sometimes you will find that you must work vertically instead of horizontally, especially when outlining is required. If faced with this, simply change your direction and work from top to bottom. Again, at the end of the canvas, turn it around and keep stitching. As you see by the diagram, the stitch remains the same; only the direction changes. All our doll designs have outlines incorporated in them. Therefore, you frequently will be using the Continental to stitch vertically, horizontally, or in a combination to form curves.

Now that we've described the Continental stitch, may we suggest that you never use it except for outlining or for very small areas. To put it another way, pretend we never told you about this stitch. It may be easy to do, but you will suffer for it later on.

The reason that most people recommend not relying totally on this stitch is the tension it creates in the canvas. As you can see from the diagram, the yarn is constantly being pulled across the canvas strands from right to left. Consequently, the stitch tends to compress the strands in this diagonal direction causing a tension that will pull your canvas out of shape. We have found that in most cases even repeated blocking will never restore the canvas to its original shape. And since blocking is no fun to begin with, why complicate matters. This problem is especially true with our Pillow People. These little folks were meant to stand up straight. If you use the Continental, you may find that they tend to lean a little when you are finished. And what could be worse than seeing our Doc listing to the left!

The Basketweave Stitch

Although this stitch may be difficult to master at first, every effort should be made to learn and use the Basketweave. From the front this stitch looks exactly like the Continental: that is, small diagonals running across the canvas. But when viewed from the back, you see why it is called the Basketweave. The stitch produces a thick woven look on the reverse side. This pattern is more durable than the Continental and helps preserve your work for a longer time.

The major difference between the Basketweave and the Continental is the direction in which the stitch is worked. As we explained, the Continental always moves from right to left. On the other hand, the Basketweave stitch moves diagonally from the lower right to the upper left and back down again without turning the canvas around. What really happens is that the needle and yarn climb up the canvas and then back down. If you picture the vertical and horizontal canvas strands as little steps going diagonally from the bottom right to the upper left, then you may see how the needle can climb up and down these steps. You might not see this at first without visual assistance.

	42	22	20	8	6	2
41	21	19 40	7 24	5 18	1 10	4
	39	23	17 38	9 26	3 16	12
		37	25	15 36	11 28	14
			35	27	13 34	30
				33	29	32
					31	

As you study the diagram let us immediately point out the biggest stumbling block in mastering this stitch. You must always remember that you are still stitching in rows. These rows run diagonally on the canvas and not vertically or horizontally. When you work diagonally up the canvas to the top, you will end the row on a horizontal strand. Working down the canvas, you will always end on a vertical strand. Now we come to the important part. At the end of each diagonal row, you must add one Continental stitch (a horizontal on the top and a vertical on the side) before beginning another diagonal row. This extra Continental stitch "sets up" the next diagonal row and becomes the first stitch in that row. If you forget to do this important stitch, believe us, you will become completely mixed up. Now let's look at the diagram. We shall point out the Continental stitch when it appears.

To start the Basketweave, bring the needle from the back of the canvas out hole 1 and in 2. The Continental, remember, begins the same way. Now the first diagonal row must be set up. Therefore, the vertical Continental stitch is used. Come out 3 and in 4. At this point there should be two stitches. The lower one is the first stitch in the first diagonal row. When entering 4, do not put the needle all the way through. Instead, point the needle left, go under two vertical strands and come out at 5. Then go in 6. As you can see, you have completed the first diagonal row. Now you must set up the next row with one horizontal Continental stitch. Come out 7 and in 8. Again, don't pull the needle all the way through. Point the needle down, go under two horizontal strands, and come out 9. Go in 10, under two more horizontal strands, and out 11. Go in 12. Again a diagonal row is complete, and it is time to set up the next row with the vertical Continental stitch. From 12, come out 13, then in 14, go under two vertical strands, and come out 15. Then in 16 and out 17; in 18 and out 19 and in 20. Another row is complete. Once again set up the next row with a horizontal Continental: out 21 and in 22, then downward, coming out at 23 and in 24. We could go on forever, but there is no need to because the stitch is repetitive.

Now that we have told you how to start the Basketweave, it would be a good idea to tell you how to stop it or at least contain it so you can follow design lines. Remember, you can always stop the direction of the stitch by substituting either the horizontal or vertical Continental for the Basketweave. We've already explained this with the top and the right side. The same holds true for the bottom and left side boundaries. If you want to make a side boundary, simply do one vertical Continental down and then go back in the opposite direction with the Basketweave. If you want to make a bottom boundary, just substitute the horizontal Continental. You are, then, controlling the length of the Basketweave row and the size of the boundaries by that one extra Continental stitch we said was so important. The best method of learning all this is to practice on a small piece of canvas. Just follow our diagram and instructions until you no longer need them.

All of this may sound too complicated for someone just looking for a pleasant diversion to keep the hands busy and the mind alert. But with a little patience the Basketweave can be easily mastered in a very short time. Believe it or not, we no longer can go back to relying completely on the Continental stitch. The Basketweave has become easier and faster for us.

You may ask why we are placing so much stress on a stitch that seems to be so difficult to master. There are a number of reasons. Probably the most obvious plus for the Basketweave is that you do not rotate the canvas at the end of a row. This may sound like a small matter, but it saves time and a lot of effort. The flow of your stitching will not be interrupted by the "stop and rotate" that is required with the Continental.

If you hate to block canvases as much as we do, you will really fall in love with the Basketweave. It does not distort the canvas. The reason for this again lies in the stress placed on the mesh. The tension created by stitching diagonally up the mesh is canceled by the opposing tension of the downward diagonal.

Any discussion of the Basketweave must include the finished look of your needlepoint work. We mentioned a moment ago the "flow" of stitching. Since the canvas is not rotated, most people quickly develop their own rhythm, which tends to place an even stress on the canvas. This constant tension means that your work will be uniform, unlike the bumps and ridges that seem to appear with the Continental stitch. The Basketweave gives a professional look to your completed work.

So far we have dealt with the two basic needlepoint stitches, which form diagonals over the intersection of the horizontal and vertical canvas strands. Using these two stitches, anyone can needlepoint almost any design from a bird to a sunset to a geometric. The diagonal covers an area of canvas, and the yarn color determines the finished pattern.

Occasionally, you just might want to introduce into your design a certain effect, which the diagonal stitch cannot give. This effect comes from a change in texture and produces a corresponding change in visual stimulation. In other words, if you change the stitch, you are definitely going to change the look of your work. We are going to deal with three of these "special-effects" stitches. Of course, there are loads of other stitches that the curious might turn to for some added fun. If you feel in the mood to make a change in the texture and look of our Pillow People's clothing, there are a variety of exotic stitches to choose from such as the Hungarian Ground, the Shell, Rococo, Crossed Corners, and so on. We have designed all our dolls around two very well-known stitches, the Brick and the Zigzag, and one lesser known, called Turkey Tufting, which we use for the doll's hair.

The Brick Stitch

Unlike the Continental or Basketweave, the Brick stitch works only over the horizontal strands of the canvas. This stitch is vertical. It is important to remember that the Brick will work only when it covers an *even* number of strands. In our diagram we will show the Brick covering two strands, but you can increase its size to four or even six strands.

8		6		4		2
	6A		4A		2A	
7 6		5 11		3 13		1 15
	5A 7A		3A 9A		1A 11A	
10		12		14		16 18
	8A		10A		12A	
						17

You will notice that this stitch always skips two vertical strands. This holds true no matter how many horizontal strands are covered because the vertical space provides room for building alternating rows. This stitch also works from right to left. We again begin from the back of the canvas and bring the needle out 1. Then going vertically up, skip two strands and go in 2. As with most stitches, your job will be much easier if you do not pull the needle all the way through the hole, but rather, point it toward the next hole. This saves you a lot of time and effort. Now remember to skip two vertical strands and pull the needle out at 3. Again, cover two horizontal strands and go in 4. Now simply repeat this stitch until you reach the end of your row. At this point rotate the canvas and make sure that you begin this row in the bottom hole of the last stitch (No. 7). Continue this stitch across the canvas, complete the row, and rotate the canvas. As you work this stitch, you will notice two things. First, the Brick stitch covers a lot of canvas very quickly. Second, thus far you have stitched vertical columns that alternate with vertical empty holes. You are only half done.

Once you cover as much area as you want, go back to the original starting point. The real enjoyment of the Brick stitch now begins, because you see the pattern build and you can feel the thick texture. This second stage of stitches begins in the empty hole that is diagonally down to the left of the first original hole. Therefore, the needle comes out at 1A, moves up and covers two horizontal strands, and goes in at 2A. You then repeat the whole process again until you have filled in your canvas. Once you have completed this second set, you will notice that the top and bottom rows have missing stitches caused by the alternating nature of the stitch. All that has to be done now is to fill in the exposed strands with a vertical stitch half the length of the original. In other words, stitching from right to left, cover the remaining horizontal strands on the top and bottom rows.

For a simple stitch the Brick is quite rewarding. We love to use it because it produces such a thick texture. Changing from the diagonal stitch to the Brick, you will become aware of an abrupt difference in feel. The Brick stitch almost feels like a mat. And the Brick design is very pleasing to the eye. You can, of course, change the overall look of the design by introducing different colors into the work. Instead of working the entire canvas in one color, stitch the first half in one color and the second in a complementary color. The resulting striped effect can be stunning.

A lot of people love to use the Brick stitch for backgrounds. The main reason for this is that it covers the canvas so quickly and easily. Even though we can grow lazy at times, we do not think that this stitch should be used for most background work, owing to its thickness. When this stitch is mixed in with the Continental or Basketweave, it definitely stands out farther from the canvas. Therefore, to the viewer the Brick pattern looks as though it were in the foreground instead of the background. For the purposes of this book we have restricted the use of the Brick stitch to certain pieces of clothing such as dresses, socks, and pants.

The Zigzag Stitch

We are crazy about this stitch. Besides using the Zigzag in the Pillow People, we both have rooms full of pillows stitched in this beautiful geometric design. Before explaining this stitch, we want to say something about its effect on you as a needlepoint enthusiast.

The Zigzag is a great form of therapy. If you are tired of concentrating on difficult designs, if you have had it with the world's problems, or if the kids are driving you crazy, the Zigzag is for you. It is pure and simple escapism. Once you have learned this stitch, just sit back and let it fill your canvas. Since it is based entirely on repetition, there is really nothing to think about except what colors you might want to use. And let's face it, sometimes it's wonderful not to have to think.

But now back to reality. The Zigzag is a vertical stitch that is repeated after every tenth stitch across the canvas from right to left. The Zigzag climbs diagonally up and down the canvas as it moves along the mesh. It is best to begin somewhere in the middle of the canvas. Then, once you have established the design across the middle, you can fill in to the top and bottom borders.

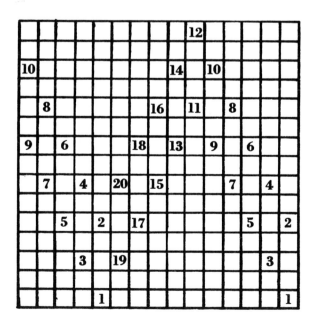

Beginning from the back of the canvas, bring the needle out hole 1. You are now going to cover the next four horizontal strands and go in at 2. Next bring your needle down two strands and out 3. Cover four horizontal strands and go in 4. Then come out 5 and in 6. Repeat this stitch three more times until you have a total of six vertical stitches running diagonally up the canvas. Now it is time to come back down to the original starting line. From hole 12, bring your needle down and under six horizontal strands and come out at 13. Then cover four strands and go in 14. Go down and under six more strands to 15, and so on. Once you have completed ten of these vertical stitches, it will be time to repeat the whole process from 1 to 20 again. Remember that the starting point for each set of ten stitches must always be on the same horizontal strand.

When you reach the left-side border, rotate the canvas and begin the steps again. Don't forget that the top hole of each stitch in one row becomes the bottom hole of each stitch in the next row. This guarantees that there will be no gaps.

As we said earlier, the best way to learn is by doing. Using an extra piece of canvas, practice the Zigzag until you understand how it covers the mesh. You will notice immediately that you cover a lot of area in a short time. When you finally get to the top and bottom areas, keep the pattern going, but shorten the length of each stitch so that all the stitches end on the same horizontal line.

We must offer one word of caution. This stitch works up so fast and is so repetitive that mistakes can be made without noticing them. Probably the biggest error is not keeping the individual stitch vertical. If you accidently put the needle in the wrong hole, either to the left or to the right, the stitch will slant and consequently throw off the pattern from that point on. So always be careful where you put your needle!

The fun of the Zigzag is not only the pattern, but the range of colors you may use. We have made some spectacular pillows by changing colors with each row. A lot of people believe that the colors should be repetitive. This can be attractive with a wise choice of colors. But we love a random assortment; the disorder adds to the wild look that we enjoy.

The Zigzag has been used in this book to add visual interest to our little people's clothing. Because it is such a dominant stitch, we have not used it often. We feel that it can pull attention away from the dolls' faces. Again, since we are talking about special-stitch effects, it should be remembered that they are special and to be used only for certain design emphasis.

The Hair Stitch

The only thing we do not like about Turkey Tufting is its name. So before we go any further, let's call it the Hair stitch. If you take a moment to look through the design section of this book, you will notice that we have put the Hair stitch to very good use. Almost all of our dolls have been given hair. Whether it's long, short, curly, or straight, the Hair stitch seems to add another dimension to the individual doll's personality. This stitch is also used to make the eyelashes or any other hair you care to add. For example, our lovable Wella Witch has a little hair on the end of her nose and chin.

The Hair stitch is very, very easy to learn. It can also drive you crazy. But first things first. Let's turn to a diagram for visual help. This stitch is made up entirely of loops that are tied down. Each loop becomes its own little knot, which keeps the doll's hair from falling out or being pulled out. As a point of interest, this stitch is also used to make rugs; so you know it is strong.

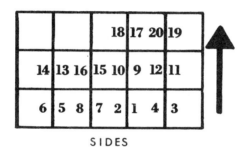

SIDES

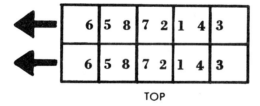

TOP

Unlike all the other stitches we have described, the Hair stitch is started from the *front* of the canvas. Put the needle in 1, go under the left vertical strand and out 2. Now, reverse direction, cover two vertical strands, and go in 3. Again, go under the left vertical strand and come out at 4, which is your original starting point, hole 1. Pull the yarn tight, and you have made your first knot. Now skip one hole and go in 5, come out 6, cross over and in 7, and out 8. Make sure you leave a loop between the first and second knots. The length of that loop determines the length of the hair. Leaving room for another loop, move up the canvas to the next horizontal row of holes. Go in 9 and out 10, in 11 and out 12. Stitch two knots and keep moving upward until you reach the top of the head. It is important to remember that there should never be any holes left between the hair and the face. Therefore, the Hair stitch closest to the face must share a hole with the diagonal stitch used for the skin.

We have discovered that a full head of hair can be achieved with only two Hair stitches per row, so there is no need to kill yourself with extra stitches. As we have mentioned, the stitch is easy but can drive you nuts. If you follow the diagram and try it, you will see why. Each stitch gets in the way of making new stitches, and you can't see the holes through the loops. This job of adding hair can be made a lot easier if you follow a few helpful hints.

First, don't even think about adding any hair until you have finished everything else. The hair must be saved until last because it sticks out from the canvas and constantly interferes with working areas nearby. We don't even suggest that you put in the eyelashes until the end. Just save a horizontal row of holes at the bottom of the eyelid for the lashes. In our designs, this row is marked with X's.

You should always work the Hair stitch from bottom to top. Again, this direction keeps completed hair from getting in the way of making new stitches. The best thing to do is make two stitches, place these loops under your thumb, and move up to the next row of holes. By doing this thumb work, you always keep the new hair under control and out of the way.

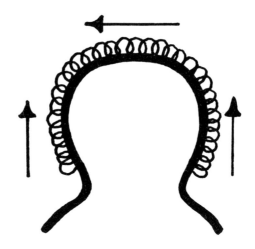

When beginning the hair, start in the lower right side of the doll's head and move up, making only two loops per row. When you reach the top, stitch one row completely across until you reach the side. Then cut the yarn and stitch another row above the first one. You now have a doll with hair on the top and one side. To fill in the remaining side, start at the bottom of the hairline and work up until you meet the hair on top. This last part can be difficult because you now must not only control the new side hair, but also the hair on top. Just keep using your thumb and forefinger to move the loops out of your way.

If you want the doll's hair to be curly, don't cut the loops. For straight hair cut all the loops after you have finished. Some of our dolls have hair about six inches long. That means you must allow for very large loops and, of course, lots of extra yarn. In other cases, such as the eyelashes, the loops should be kept small.

You can easily make the hair appear as though you have stitched two or three times as many loops. Just unravel the 3-strand yarn, making three loops out of one. It gives a much fuller and more natural look.

Our only other suggestion concerns a stitch that will never be seen when the doll is completed. When making the canvas into a pillow, you will machine-stitch the backing along the outer edges of the design. Therefore, you will need a few extra diagonal stitches around the outside of the hair for the machine to sew into. But we already said the hair should be saved until last because it gets in the way of everything else. We have got around this problem by simply turning the canvas over and stitching on the back where there is no hair. This rim, incidentally, need be only two or three diagonal stitches per row. Keep in mind that this stitch is for the machine and not you. When the doll is finished and turned right-side-out, it will be on the inside with the stuffing.

We would like to say one last thing about all the stitches described so far. They are not nearly as difficult as they sound at first. Once you have tried each stitch, learn how to make your fingers move and which way to point the needle; the stitches will become not only familiar but second nature to you. Remember what we said at the beginning. Needlepoint should be fun.

2
How to Use This Book

In school we were all told by our teachers not to copy. This chapter is devoted to the opposite dictum. On the following pages you will find designs for all our Pillow People that, we hope, you will copy, transfer to a canvas, and enjoy making into a finished pillow.

The beauty of working with our designs is that you don't have to know how to draw. We have friends who cannot even draw a straight line, much less people, and they have turned out fantastic dolls. All you have to know is how to count. We have drawn the Pillow People on a graph and the graph corresponds exactly to the No. 10 canvas. In other words, both the graph and the canvas have ten vertical and ten horizontal lines per inch. You will also notice that these lines make up ten holes per inch or a hundred holes per square inch.

Preparing the Canvas

After you have selected a design, the first step should be cutting the canvas to the approximate size of the doll. To determine this size, simply count the number of holes across the design for the width and the number from top to bottom for the length.

Remember to give yourself a few extra inches around the border for blocking purposes. Again, looking at our designs, you will see that each one has a middle mark indicated by an arrow at the top. This mark will be your guide to transferring the design onto the canvas accurately.

The arrow points to the middle line that runs down the center of the design. The best way to transfer the pattern is to work line by line from top to bottom. Just start at the middle line and count outward the number of vertical lines until you reach the outline. This count must be done on both the right and the left sides or you will end up with a one-sided doll. This method allows you to pinpoint the location of the design wherever it crosses a vertical strand.

By folding your canvas in half vertically, you can find the middle strand, which you should mark for easy identification. Now you are ready to start working: first count out the graph lines until you meet the outline, then count out the canvas strands from the middle and make a mark. As you move line by line down the canvas, the design will appear.

This count method is accurate but can be time-consuming. You might want to transfer the design, using a ruler. In this case all you do is measure from the center to the outline of the design and double it. The designs are about one-half the size of the actual doll. If the pattern measures two inches, just measure four inches off on the canvas from the center strand outward and place a mark. The ruler method is not as accurate a means of strand count, but it is a lot faster and saves considerable strain on the eyes.

The easiest way to transfer a design is by taking the pattern to a store that makes photostats. Have the design blown up to twice its size. You will use this photostat to transfer the design onto your canvas. This is accomplished by putting a piece of nonsmudge carbon paper between the photostat and the canvas and tracing the design onto the mesh. If you can get to a photostat store, this method really makes sense: it is easy yet accurate.

There are one or two areas in the design where you should strive for perfection. This comes more as a helpful hint than as a definite rule. We have learned from experience that the eyes and the mouth are the most important single design elements because their shape determines the doll's whole personality and look. You will find that it pays to spend a little extra time accurately transferring them to your canvas. This same care should be shown when you actually begin to needlepoint. Start with the eyes and the mouth. If you don't like what you stitch, or if you want to make a change in either area, this is the time to do it; not later when whole areas might have to be cut out to make the same change.

Have you ever worked months on a needlepoint project, just to learn that it was ruined because the design was not drawn with a waterproof marker? It has happened to us, and it can be heartbreaking. Don't let it happen to you. There are different ways of drawing on canvas without worrying that the outline will bleed through the yarn during blocking. The professionals use oil or acrylic paints. But for our purposes the easiest and cheapest method is to use a waterproof marker pen. You can buy markers that have been specially made for needlecraft work. We do recommend, however, that you test a small piece of canvas with the marker first. After making a large dot on the mesh, place it in a glass of water for a minute or so. If the dot does not smudge, you know the marker is safe to use.

As you draw the design on the canvas, be sure to follow your marks and to keep the marker point on the canvas strand. Often the point tends to fall off the strand into the holes and actually ends up marking two strands instead of one. This double line may cause some confusion when you get around to stitching the area. Since we seem to be offering a lot of suggestions, here's another. Use a light color marker for your work. Sometimes the dark colors show through the lighter yarn colors and give your work a very sloppy look.

We have included a photograph of the completed doll next to the design. This should serve as an extra guide for you while transferring the design by allowing you to see what certain areas will look like when finished. Some people even find it easier to use both the graph and the photograph when they are drawing. One seems to aid the other.

Color Selection

Each design also comes with a list of suggested yarn colors to use when stitching. If you want to duplicate the coloration of our dolls, just follow the color index. We have tried to list every color and where it is needed within the design. As we said earlier, however, everyone has his own favorite colors, and we encourage you to use whatever you like best. The only exception to this may be the skin tone. It is best not to use pure white unless you want a very flat, unnatural look. Also, if you go too far into the pinks, the skin can begin to look as though it is burned. The best thing to do is ask the salesperson at your store to show you several shades of flesh color. You will need two shades, one light for the skin and one darker for the outlines.

There should be only a few places where an outline is ever needed. As you will see, we always outline the arms and hands in a dark flesh color. Or if the doll has a shirt or blouse, the sleeves will be outlined to distinguish them from the same-colored shirt. But as a general rule you should try to do as little outlining as possible. The different colors provide the contrast and make their own borders. If you think that colors next to each other are too much the same, you may either outline or change one of the colors. And please, never, never outline around the eyes. The dolls will suddenly take on a very evil and menacing look. One of the few dolls with outlined eyes is Wella Witch, and this was done purposely to make her a little frightening. If any special outlining is required, we will make note of it in the color index.

And last of all, what about those special-effect stitches we discussed earlier? Well, don't worry. We will tell you when and where to use them. Now it is time to begin. Pick one of the Pillow People and have a ball!

3

The Pillow People Designs

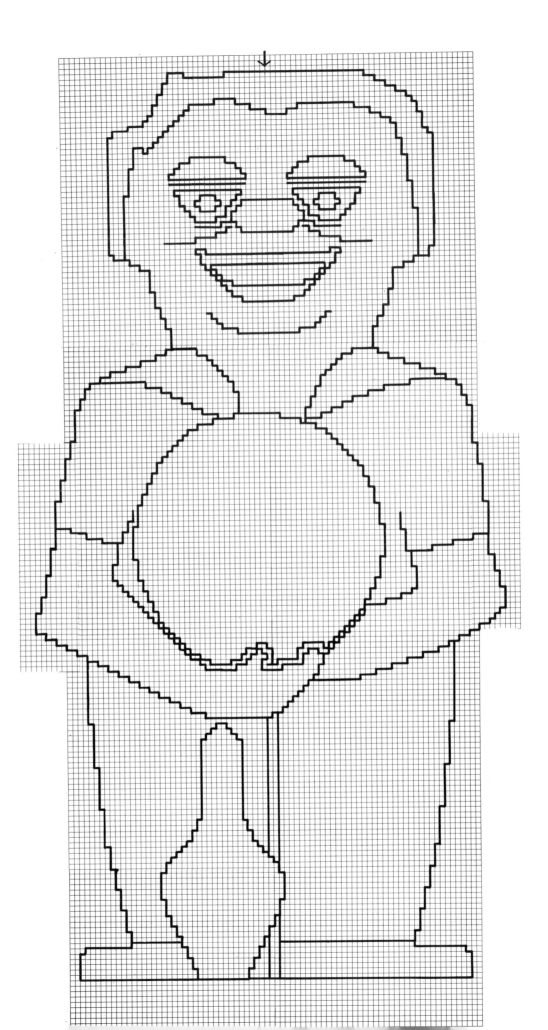

Bernie Bowler

STITCH
Continental or Basketweave

YARN COLORS
Hair: *brown*
Skin: *flesh*
Eyelids: *gray*
Lash line: *dark gray*
Eyeballs: *pale blue*
Eyes: *white*
Nose: *medium pink*
Lips: *red*
Teeth: *white*
Shirt: *gold*
Piping: *light green*
Arm outline: *medium pink*
Bowling ball: *black*
Pants: *brown*
Bowling pin: *white*
Shoes: *red*
Pantleg divider: *dark brown*

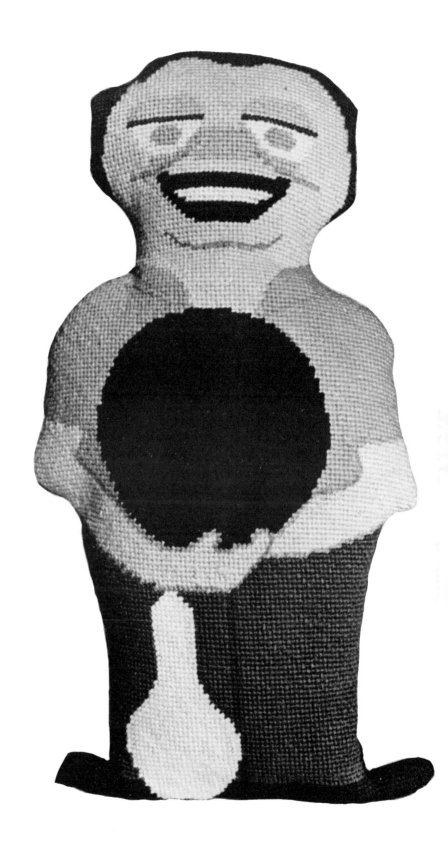

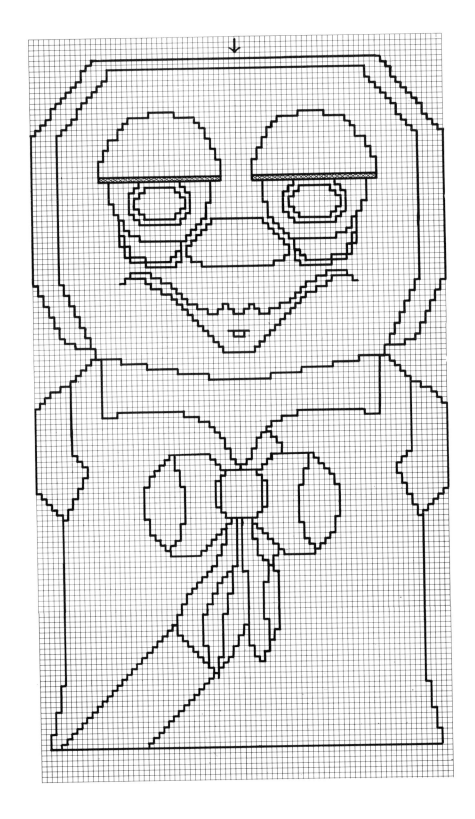

Syrupy Shirley

STITCHES
Continental or Basketweave; Hair

YARN COLORS
Hair: *dark gray*
Skin: *flesh*
Eyelids: *medium blue*
Lashes: *black*
Eyeballs: *chocolate brown*
Eyes: *white*
Eyeball outline: *black*
Nose: *shocking pink*
Rouge: *medium orange*
Lips: *brilliant red*
Lip opening: *shocking pink*
Body: *light pink*
Dress, right: *medium yellow*
Dress, left: *red*
Bow: *light and dark green*

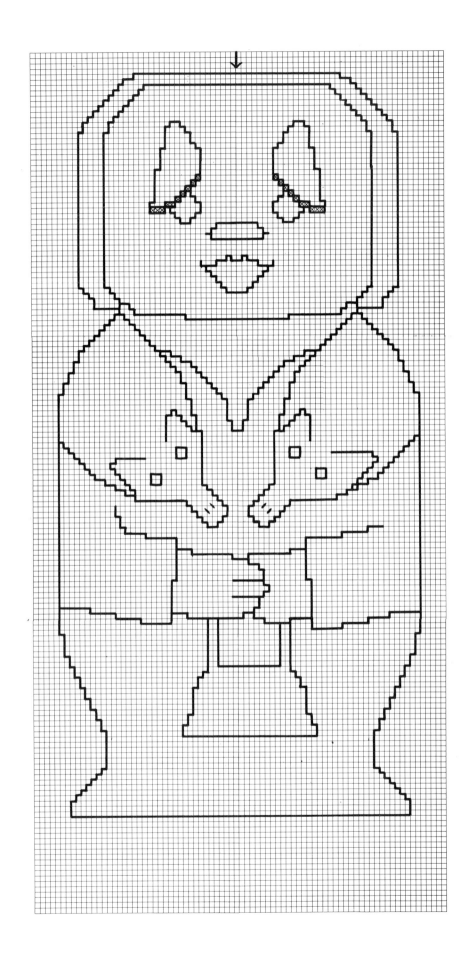

32

Elegant Edythe

STITCHES
Continental or Basketweave; Hair

YARN COLORS
Hair: *dark brown*
Skin: *light pink*
Eyelids: *bright green*
Eyelashes: *bright green*
Eyeballs: *medium blue*
Nose: *medium pink*
Lips: *red*
Skin outline: *medium pink*
Dress: *gold*
Fox boa: *angora brown*
Hands: *skin pink*
Arm outline: *black*
Pocketbook: *medium green*

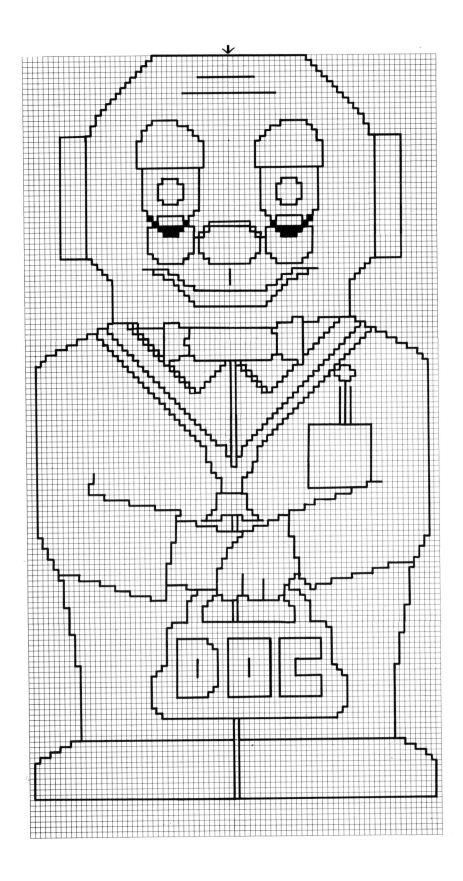

34

Doc

STITCHES
Continental or Basketweave; Hair

YARN COLORS
Hair: *light gray*
Skin: *flesh*
Eyelids: *dark gray*
Eyeballs: *medium blue*
Eyes: *white*
Glasses: *black*
Eyebags: *medium pink*
Nose: *peach*
Lips: *red*
Bowtie: *gold with brown outline*
Jacket: *medium blue*
Jacket outline: *dark blue*
Stethoscope: *brown and black*
Thermometer: *white with red center*
Hands: *flesh with pink outline*
Pants: *brown*
Bag: *black*
Letters: *white*
Shoes: *white*

36

Jesse

STITCHES
Continental or Basketweave; Hair

YARN COLORS
Hair: *brown*
Eyelids: *gold*
Eyeballs: *brown*
Eyes: *white*
Nose: *dark pink*
Face: *flesh*
Lips: *red*
Teeth: *white*
Scarf: *gold*
Buckle: *red*
Shirt outline: *black*
Shirt: *forest green*
Star: *silver*
Belt: *dark gold*
Belt buckle outline: *black*
Guns: *black*
Holsters: *gold*
Chaps: *brown*
Boots: *dark gold*

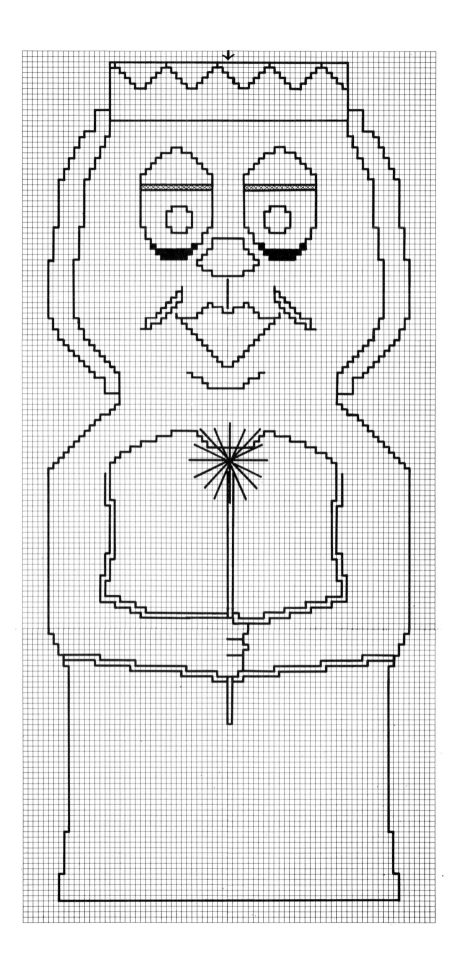

The Princess

STITCHES
Continental or Basketweave; Hair; 1½-
   inch-long stitches to form radiating
   star effect

YARN COLORS
Crown: *gold thread*
Hair: *sunny yellow*
Skin: *flesh*
Skin outline: *dark flesh*
Eyelids: *purple*
Eyelashes: *yellow and gold thread*
Eyeballs: *blue*
Eyes: *white*
Eyebags: *shocking pink*
Nose and cheek outline: *medium pink*
Lips: *red*
Dress: *white with gold thread*
Wand: *gold*
Star: *gold thread*

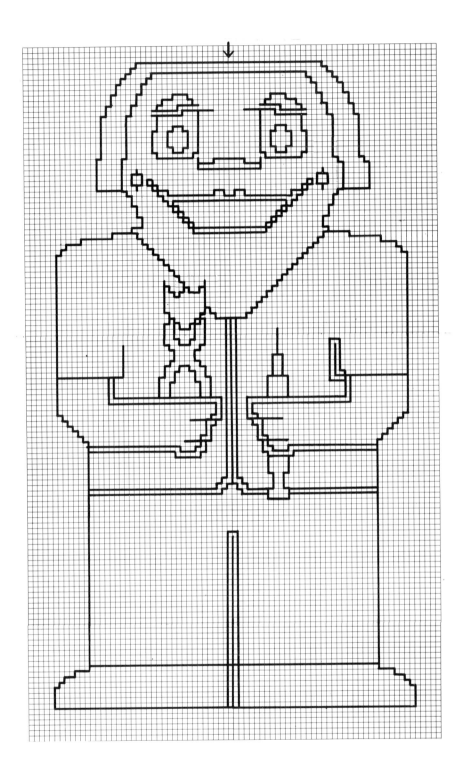

Harry the Painless Dentist

STITCHES
Continental or Basketweave; Hair

YARN COLORS
Hair: *maroon*
Eyelids: *purple*
Lashes: *black*
Eyeballs: *dark blue*
Eyes: *white*
Skin: *flesh*
Nose: *apricot*
Lips: *red*
Teeth: *white*
Jacket: *light blue*
Jacket outline: *dark blue*
Pliers: *gray with dark gray outline*
Tooth: *white with black outline*
Pants: *maroon*
Shoes: *white*

Baby Doll

STITCHES
Continental or Basketweave; Hair; Brick
   stitch for blanket

YARN COLORS
Hair curl: *flesh*
Skin: *flesh*
Eyelids: *bright pink*
Eyelashes: *flesh*
Eyeballs: *bright blue*
Eye outline: *yellow*
Nose: *bright pink*
Lips: *red*
Blanket collar: *white*
Blanket: *medium pink*
Flower petals: *bright yellow*
Flower center: *brown*

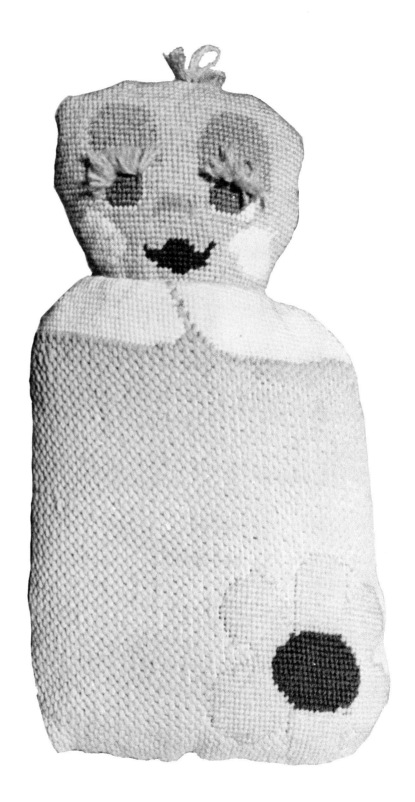

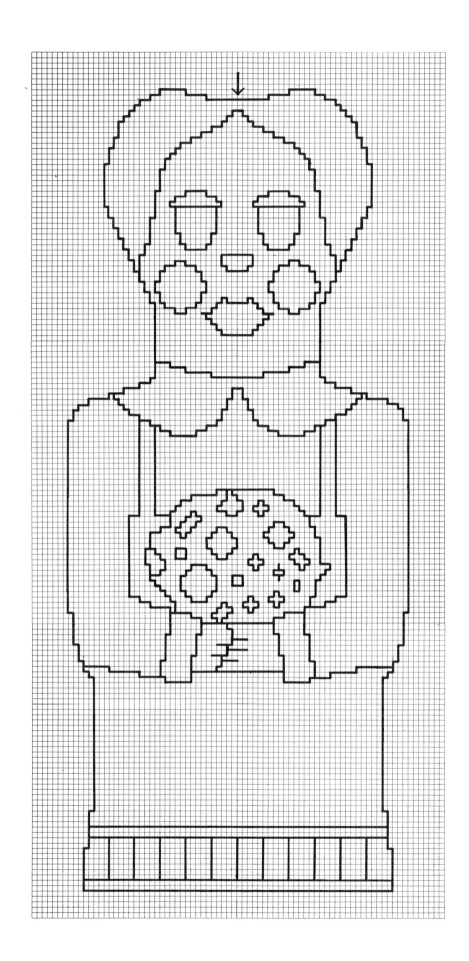

44

Lydia

STITCH
Continental or Basketweave

YARN COLORS
Hair: *chocolate brown*
Skin: *flesh*
Eyelids: *dark gray*
Nose: *dark pink*
Eyeballs: *dark blue*
Rouge and lips: *red*
Collar: *white*
Dress bodice: *shocking pink*
Sleeves: *dark pink*
Jumper and skirt: *bright orange*
Dress border: *shocking pink and bright
    blue with dark gray dividers*
Flowers: *light green background with
    multicolored flowers*

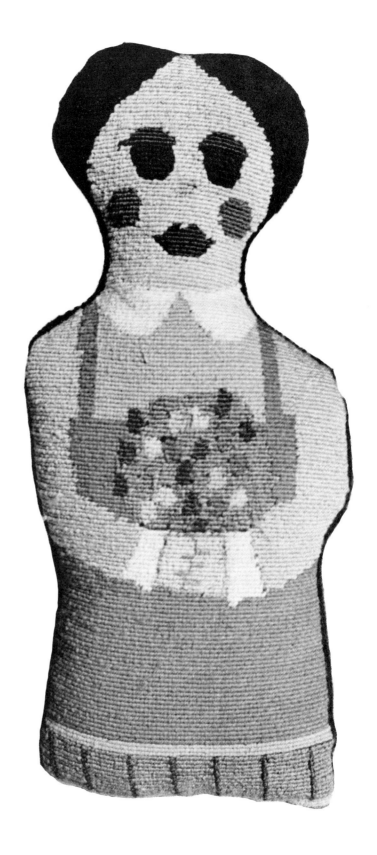

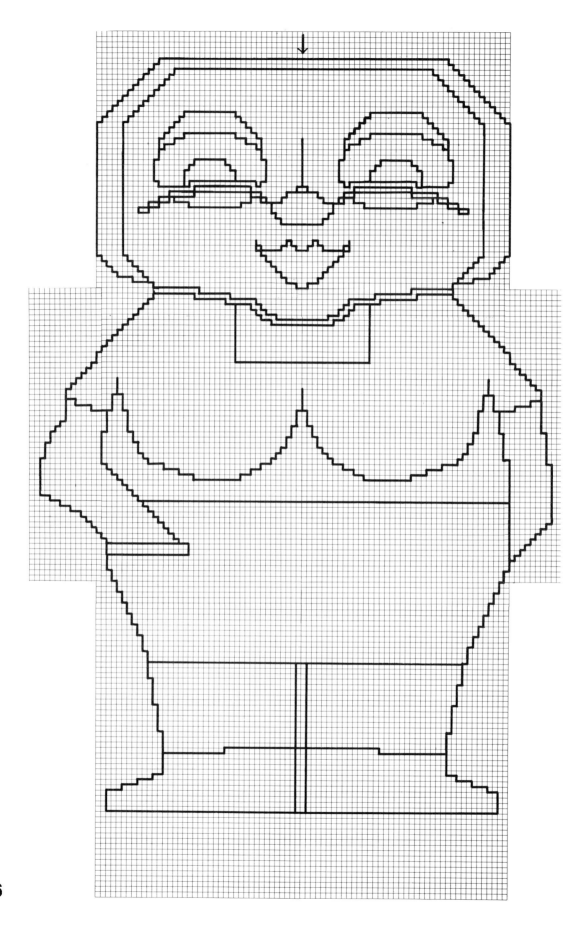

Big Mama

STITCHES

Continental or Basketweave; Hair; Brick
  stitch for blouse; Zigzag for skirt

YARN COLORS

Hair: *bright yellow*
Skin: *flesh*
Eyelids: *light lavender*
Eyes: *white*
Eyeballs: *bright blue*
Cheek outline and nose: *light red*
Lips: *red*
Chin outline: *pale orange*
Eyebags: *pale orange*
Blouse: *red*
Bosom outline: *green*
Midsection: *dark gold*
Pocket outline: *black*
Skirt: *yellow, light green, dark green*
Stockings: *flesh*
Leg divider: *light orange*
Shoes: *medium brown with dark brown
  divider*

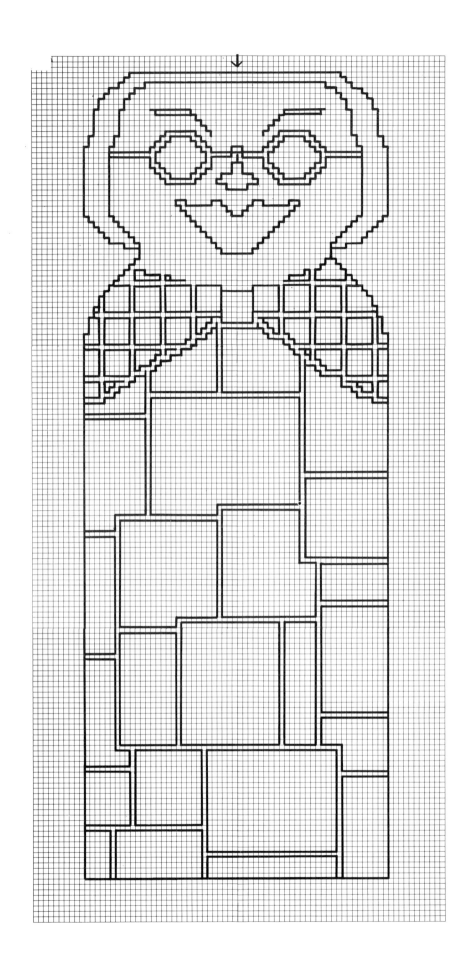

48

Quilted Bea

STITCHES

Continental or Basketweave; Hair: The
skirt area has been left up to you to
design your own patchwork pattern.
There are innumerable beautiful and
interesting stitches to choose in filling
up the area.

YARN COLORS

Hair: *dark red*
Eyebrows: *dark brown*
Glasses: *black*
Glass: *light blue*
Nose: *dark pink*
Lips: *red*
Skin: *flesh*
Dress: *all colors*

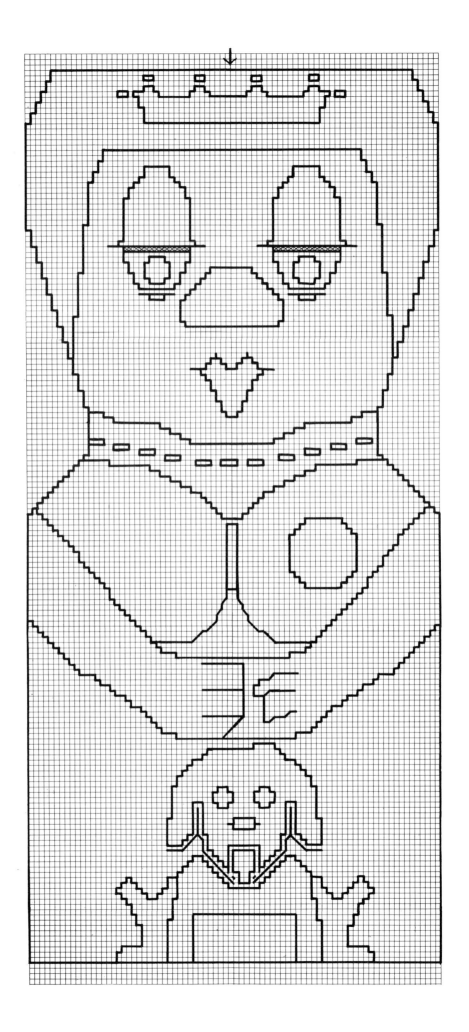

The Countess

STITCH
Continental or Basketweave

YARN COLORS
Hair: *dark gray*
Tiara: *gold with white dividers*
Skin: *flesh*
Eyelids: *royal blue*
Eyelashes: *royal purple*
Eyeballs: *brown*
Eyes: *light beige*
Eyebags: *light lavender*
Nose: *pink*
Mouth: *red*
Jawline: *pink*
Beads: *white*
Bolero jacket: *dark gold*
Pin and bolero divider: *bright gold*
Dress and skirt: *dark green*
Hands: *pink*
Dog: *browns*
Tongue: *red*
Ear and face outline: *light gray*

Liza

STITCHES
Continental or Basketweave; Hair

YARN COLORS
Hair: *bright red*
Skin: *flesh*
Eyelids: *purple*
Eyelashes: *brown*
Eyeballs: *blue*
Nose and rouge: *bright pink*
Lips: *red*
Collar: *white*
Blouse: *bright gold*
Jerkin: *dark blue*
Flower: *red*
Pants: *light green with blue divider*
Shoes: *black*
Arms: *flesh*

54

Selma and Her Doll

STITCHES
Continental or Basketweave; Hair

YARN COLORS
Hair: *maroon*
Eyebrows: *black*
Eyelids: *bright pink*
Eyelashes: *maroon*
Eyes: *white*
Eyeballs: *black*
Nose: *bright pink*
Rouge and lips: *red*
Collar: *white with red dots*
Blouse: *lemon yellow*
Skin: *pink*
Hand outline: *dark pink*
Blouse outline: *black*
Pants: *bright orange with pink divider*
Shoes: *pink*
Doll: *maroon hair; pink skin; black
    eyes; red mouth; orange legs; gray
    doll dress*

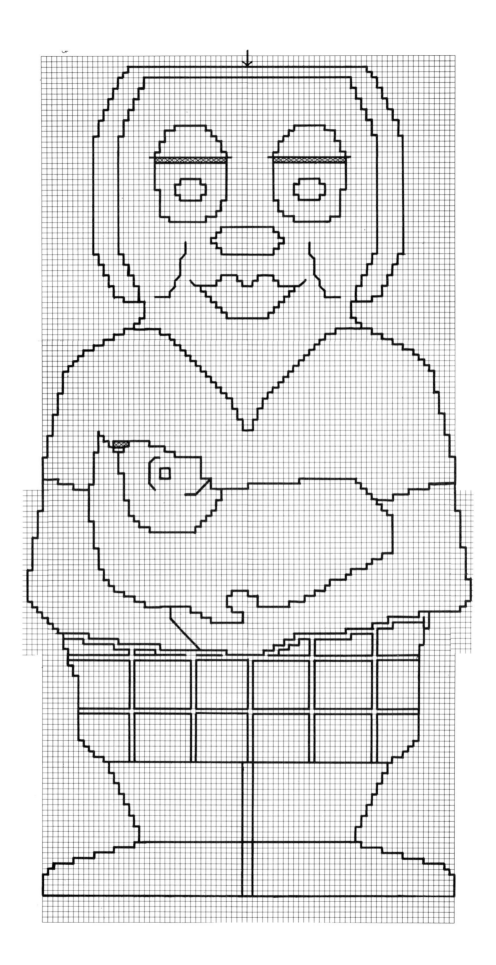

Sally with Child

STITCHES
Continental or Basketweave; Hair;
  stockings in Brick stitch

YARN COLORS
Hair: *brown*
Eyelids: *bright blue*
Eyelashes: *black*
Eyeballs: *brown*
Eyes: *white*
Skin: *flesh*
Nose and cheek lines: *bright pink*
Lips: *red*
Blouse: *lemon yellow*
Skirt: *checked orange and green*
Hand outline: *brown*
Stockings: *flesh*
Shoes: *brown*
Baby: *flesh face; brown eye and
  eyebrow; brown curl; pink blanket*

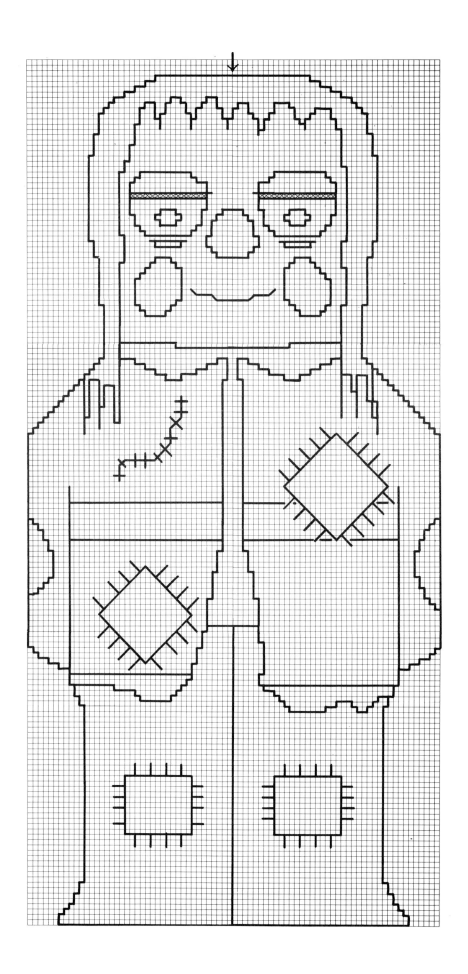

The Monster

STITCHES
Continental or Basketweave; Brick stitch
   in patches

YARN COLORS
Hair: *chocolate brown*
Skin: *flesh*
Eyelids: *blue*
Eyeballs: *brown*
Eyelashes: *dark brown*
Eyes: *white*
Eyebags: *purple*
Nose: *bright pink*
Lips and cheeks: *dark pink*
Collar and blouse: *red*
Jacket and pants: *any color*
Patches: *red, green, yellow, pink*

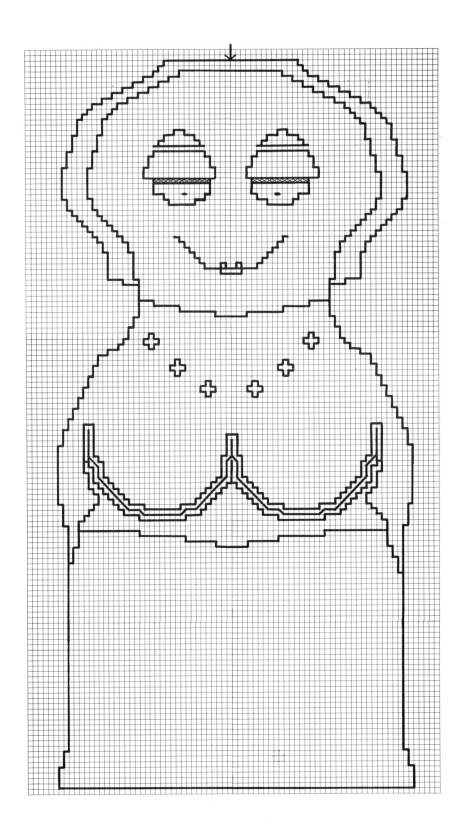

Bernice Bargello

STITCHES
Continental or Basketweave; Hair;
    blouse with Brick stitch; skirt with
    Zigzag

YARN COLORS
Hair: *yellow*
Skin: *flesh*
Eyeballs: *brown with white dot*
Eyelashes: *black*
Eyelids: *gray and lavender*
Mouth: *red*
Blouse: *pink*
Beads: *white*
Bust outline: *dark red*
Cummerbund: *green*
Skirt: *any contrasting colors*

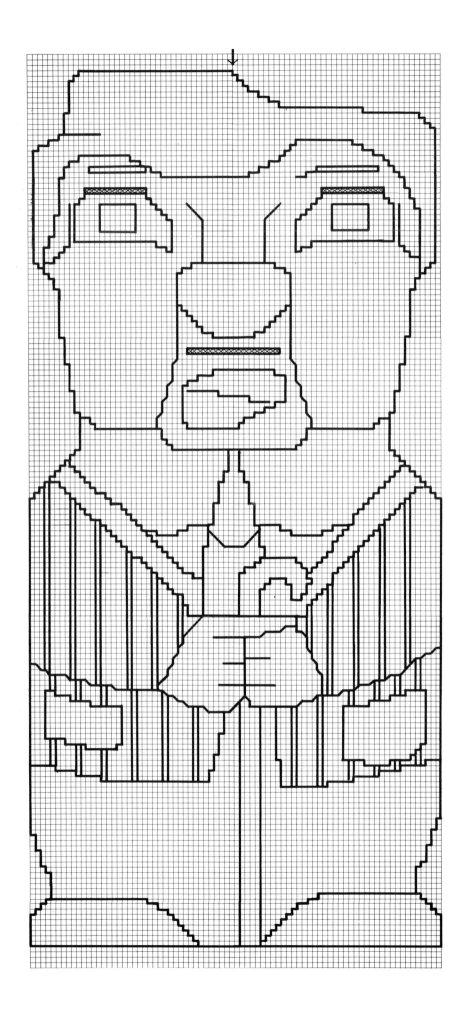

Uncle Gus

STITCH
Continental or Basketweave

YARN COLORS
Hair: *bright red*
Eyebrows: *brown*
Skin: *flesh*
Nose: *medium pink*
Mouth: *pink with red line*
Mustache: *brown*
Collar: *white*
Tie: *bright orange with gold divider*
Shirt: *medium blue*
Cane: *gold*
Hands: *flesh with black outline*
Pockets: *black*
Lapels: *black*
Jacket: *gold and green stripes*
Shoes: *black*
Pants: *blue*

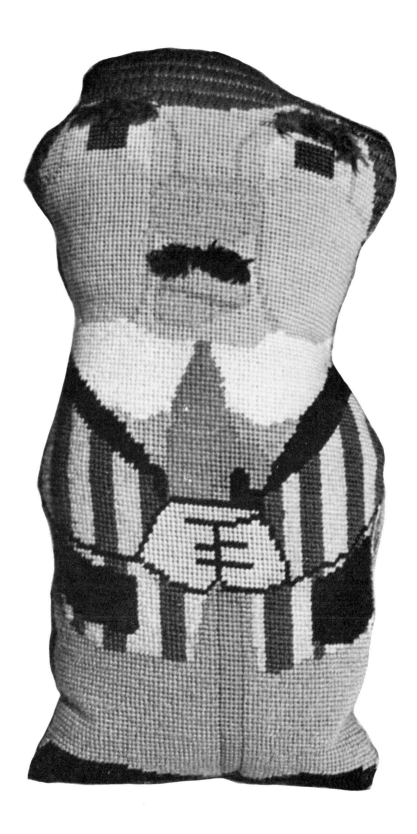

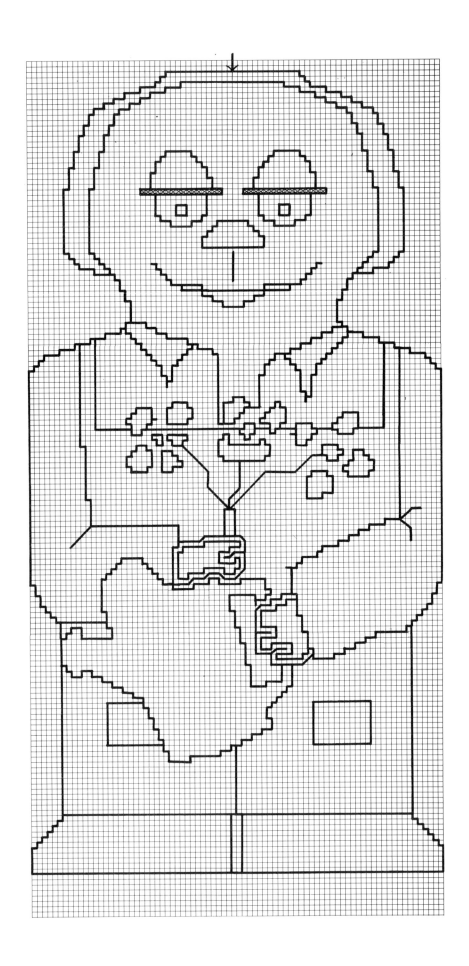

The Gardener

STITCHES
Continental or Basketweave; Hair

YARN COLORS
Hair: *brown*
Skin: *flesh*
Nose: *bright pink*
Eyelids: *bright blue*
Eyelashes: *bright blue*
Eyeballs: *brown*
Eyes: *white*
Mouth: *red*
Collar: *white*
Shirt: *brown*
Hands: *flesh with pink outline*
Flowers: *light green*
Watering can: *red*
Patches: *brown*
Overalls: *bright blue*
Shoes: *brown*

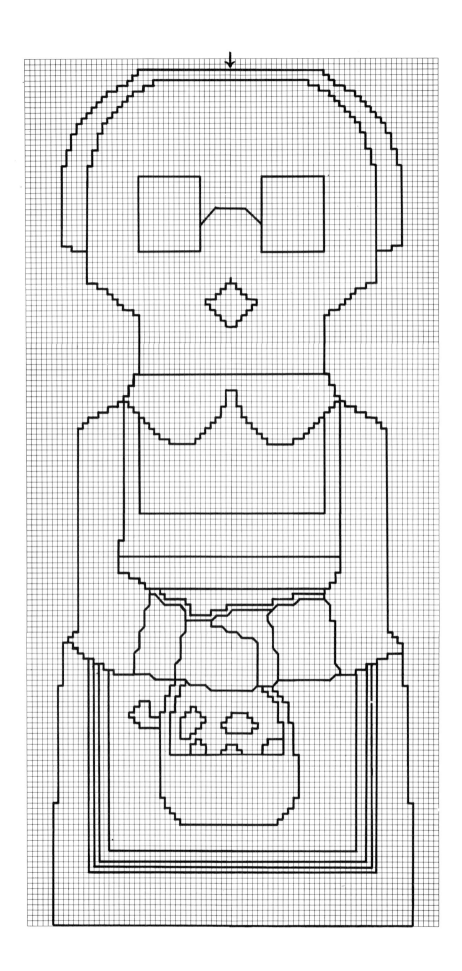

Priscilla

STITCHES
Continental or Basketweave; Hair

YARN COLORS
Hair: *dark gray*
Skin: *flesh*
Glasses: *black frames and purple glass*
Hair ties: *green*
Mouth: *shocking pink*
Collar: *white*
Dress: *shocking pink*
Apron top: *dark and light green stripes*
Hand outline: *black*
Basket: *dark red*
Flowers: *green background with any
    color flowers*
Apron bottom: *orange with blue border*
Skirt: *medium green*

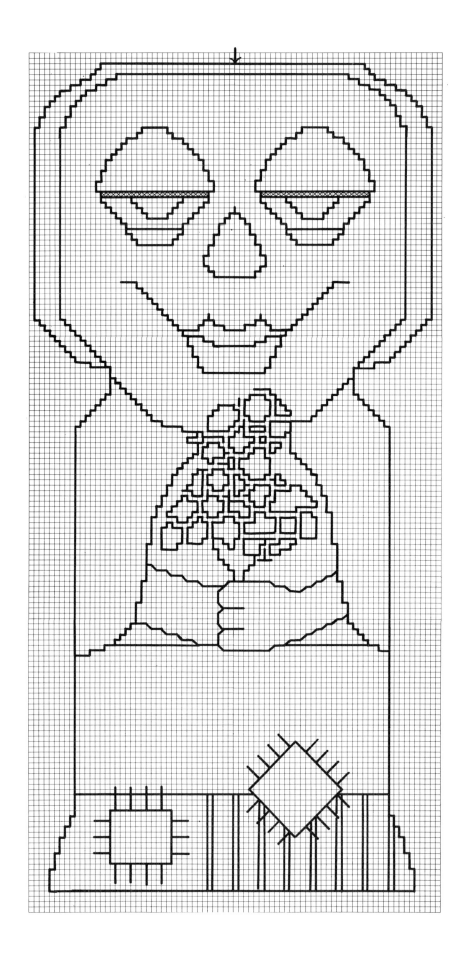

Apple Annie

Continental or Basketweave; Hair

YARN COLORS
Hair: *beige*
Skin: *beige*
Eyelids: *royal blue*
Eyelashes: *royal blue*
Eyeballs: *brown*
Eyes: *white*
Eyebags: *dark gray*
Nose: *bright pink*
Lips: *light and dark red*
Shawl: *dark blue*
Hands: *beige with peach outline*
Blouse: *gold*
Flowers: *all colors with green stem*
Skirt: *various browns*

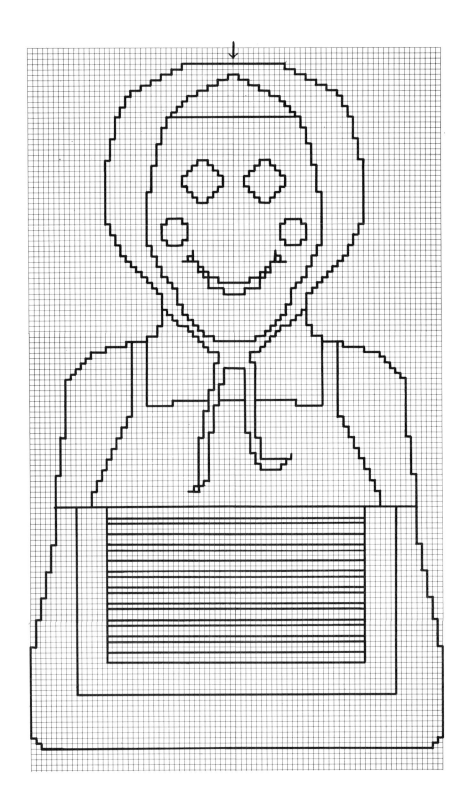

The Farmer's Wife

STITCH
Continental or Basketweave

YARN COLORS
Bandanna: *bright orange*
Hair: *bright yellow*
Eyes: *bright blue*
Rouge: *medium pink*
Lips: *red*
Skin: *beige*
Blouse: *brown*
Jerkin: *light tan*
Skirt: *green*
Apron: *dark and light pink in rows*

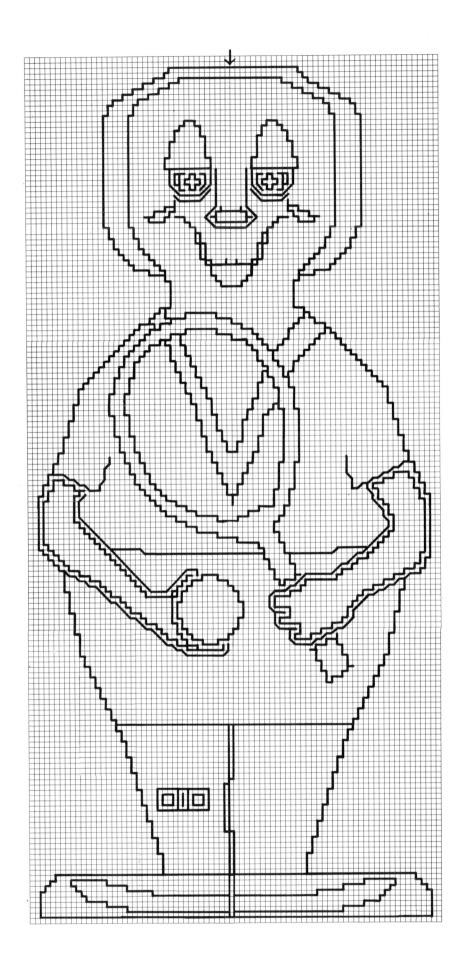

72

Tennis Player

STITCHES
Continental or Basketweave; Hair

YARN COLORS
Hair: *brown*
Skin: *flesh*
Eyelids: *purple*
Eyes: *white*
Eyeballs: *blue*
Nose and eye outline: *lavender*
Cheeks: *shocking pink*
Mouth: *red*
Racquet: *brown*
Ball: *light green*
Sweater border: *royal blue*
Skin outline: *pink*
Waistline: *dark gray*
Legs: *flesh*
Leg divider: *pink*
Bandage: *gray and white*
Shoes: *red and yellow*

73

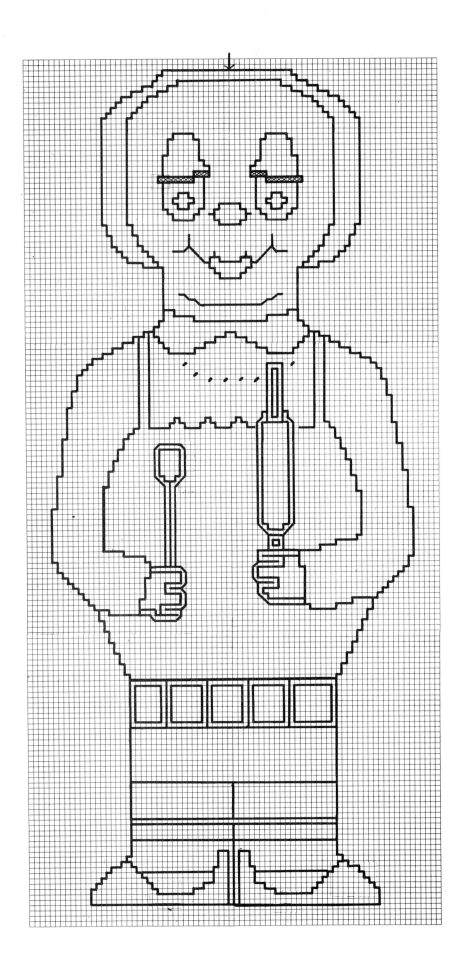

74

Bertha Baker

STITCHES
Continental or Basketweave; Hair

YARN COLORS
Hair: *bright yellow*
Eyelashes: *brown*
Eyelids: *bright pink*
Eyeballs: *blue*
Eyes: *light gray*
Lips and cheek lines: *red*
Chin line: *pink*
Nose: *pink*
Skin: *flesh*
Collar: *dark gold*
Beads: *red*
Blouse: *green*
Hands: *flesh with pink outline*
Spoon: *gold with brown outline*
Rolling pin: *gold with brown outline*
Apron: *bright yellow*
Apron border: *pink with green outline*
Legs: *flesh with pink divider*
Socks: *yellow and green stripe*
Shoes: *brown*

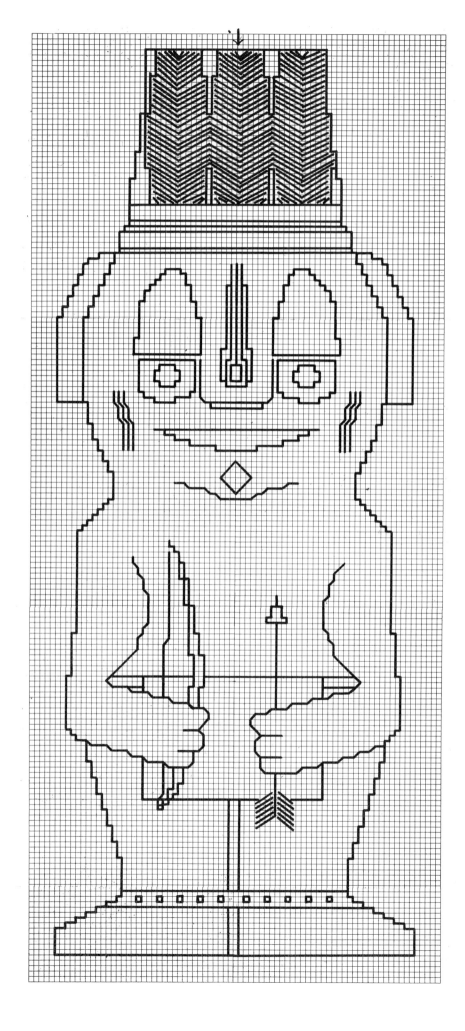

Little Brave

STITCHES

Continental or Basketweave; Hair; loin
cloth with Brick stitch; feathers are
long diagonal stitches passing over 7
to 9 vertical strands and 3 horizontal
strands

YARN COLORS

Feathers: *any bright colors*
Headband: *brown with turquoise*
  outline
Hair: *black*
Skin: *light orange*
Warpaint for nose, cheeks, and chin: *red*
  and yellow
Nose outline: *dark orange*
Eyelids: *gray*
Eyes: *white*
Eyeballs: *brown*
Mouth: *pink*
Chin and arm outline: *dark orange*
Bow: *black*
Arrow: *brown with gray point, orange*
  feathers
Loincloth: *brown*
Moccasins: *brown with purple and*
  turquoise border

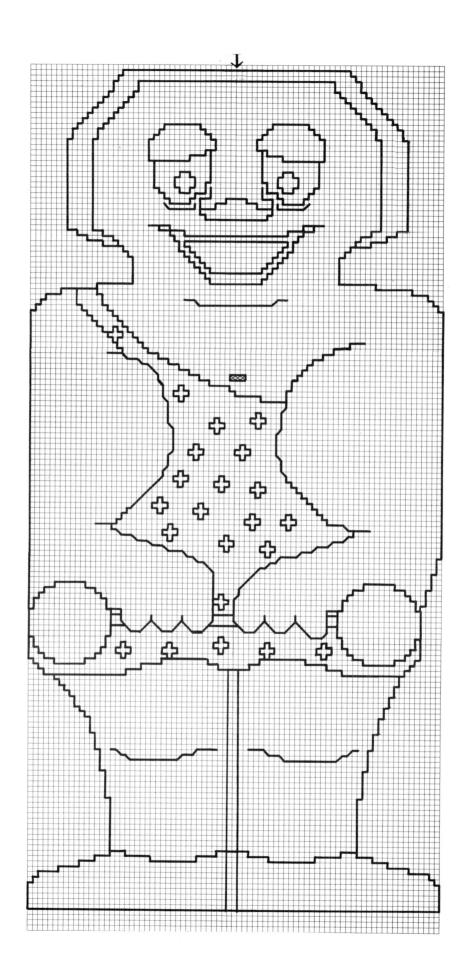

78

Muscles Morris

STITCH
Continental or Basketweave

YARN COLORS
Hair: *yellow*
Skin: *flesh*
Eyelids: *dark brown*
Eyeballs: *royal blue*
Eyes: *white*
Eye outline: *red*
Nose: *pink*
Lips: *red*
Teeth: *white*
Chin line: *pink*
Leg divider: *pink*
Knees: *pink*
Leopard skin: *gold with brown spots*
Leopard skin outline: *gray*
Barbells: *black*
Shoes: *brown*
Chest hair: *yellow*

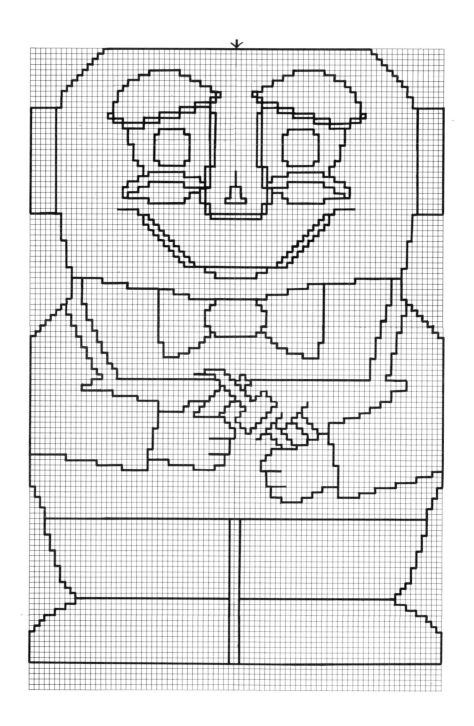

Mr. Fixit

STITCHES

Continental or Basketweave; Hair; pants
   with Brick stitch

YARN COLORS

Hair: *gray*
Skin: *flesh*
Eyelids: *gold*
Lash line: *lavender*
Eyes: *white*
Eyeballs: *blue*
Cheek line: *pink*
Nose outline: *lavender*
Mouth: *red*
Bowtie: *green with orange outline*
Shirt: *gold*
Apron: *yellow*
Hammer: *brown with gray head*
Nails: *gray*
Hands: *flesh with pink outline*
Pants: *red and pink*
Shoes: *brown*
Leg divider: *green*

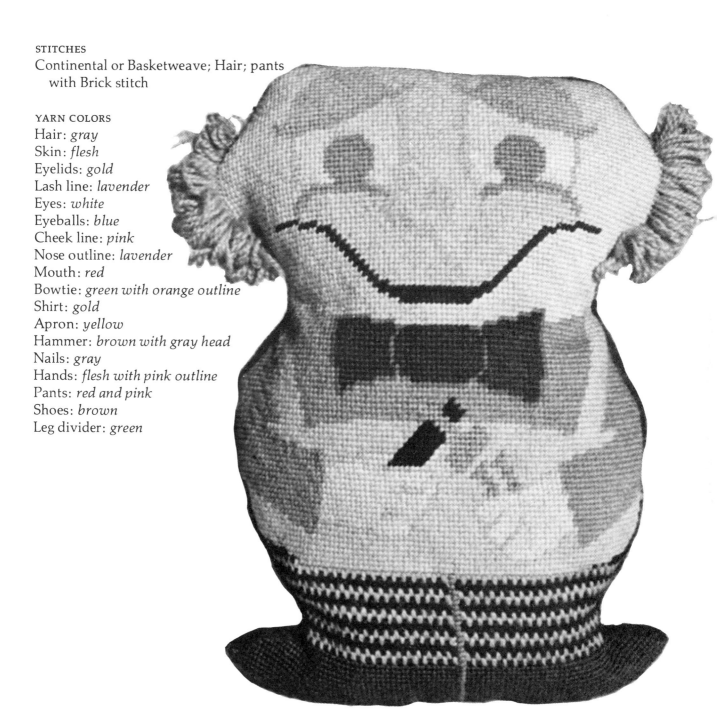

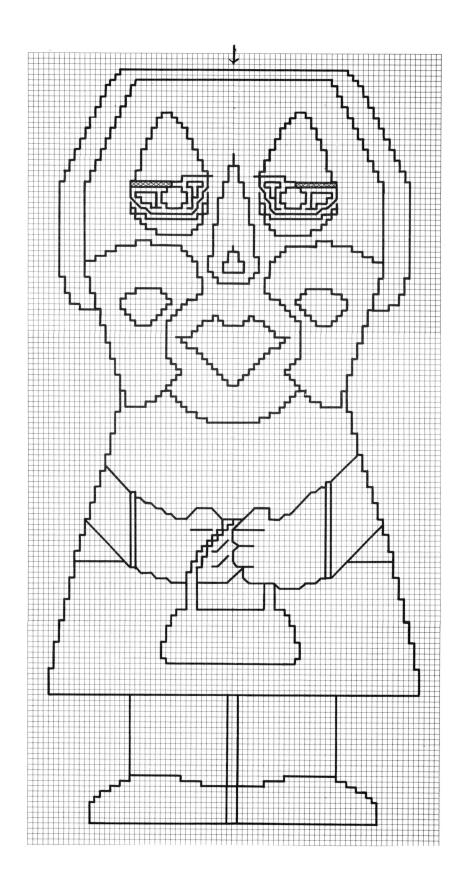

Painted Lady

STITCHES
Continental or Basketweave; Hair; skirt
  with Brick stitch

YARN COLORS
Hair: *red*
Skin: *flesh*
Eyelids: *blue*
Eyeballs: *royal blue*
Lashes: *black*
Eyebags: *blue and white, mixed*
Nose: *light pink*
Cheeks: *red*
Rouge: *dark red*
Lips: *red*
Blouse: *one-line stripes of any color*
Blouse sleeves: *one-line diagonal stripes
  of any color*
Skirt: *black*
Pocketbook: *gold*
Hands: *flesh with pink outline*
Legs: *flesh with pink divider*
Shoes: *dark blue with black divider*

Chiquita

STITCHES
Continental or Basketweave; Hair; the
   sarong in Zigzag

YARN COLORS
Fruit hat: *red apple; purple grapes with
   blue outline; yellow banana with
   brown and lemon colored lines;
   yellow lemon; green leaves in
   background; orange orange with
   brown stem*
Hair curl: *brown*
Eyebrows: *brown*
Eyelids: *dark blue*
Eyelashes: *brown*
Eye outline: *brown*
Eyes: *white*
Eyeballs: *blue*
Cheeks: *pink*
Lips: *red*
Teeth: *white with brown lines*
Flower: *yellow, gold, red, and pink*
Maracas: *dark brown*
Sarong: *yellows and greens with yellow
   border*
Sleeves: *royal blue with white cuffs*
Stockings: *blue*
Shoes: *royal blue*
Face: *flesh*
Nose: *darker flesh*
Chest: *darker flesh*
Hands: *flesh with pink outlines*
Leg divider: *white*
Space between heels and sole: *brown*
Hatband: *yellow*

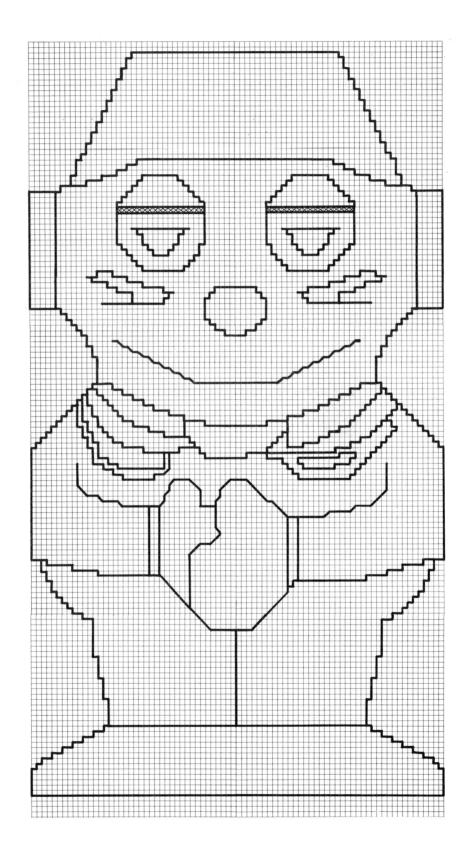

86

Lonesome Larry

STITCHES
Continental or Basketweave; Hair

YARN COLORS
Hair: *light brown*
Cap: *lemon yellow*
Skin: *pink*
Eyelids: *royal blue*
Eyelashes: *light brown*
Eyeballs: *royal blue*
Eyes: *beige*
Nose: *dark pink*
Cheeks: *medium pink*
Lips: *red*
Muffler: *yellow, royal blue, orange,
  green, and red*
Jacket: *forest green with light green arm
  outline*
Mittens: *yellow with orange outline*
Pants: *light brown with green divider*
Shoes: *blue*

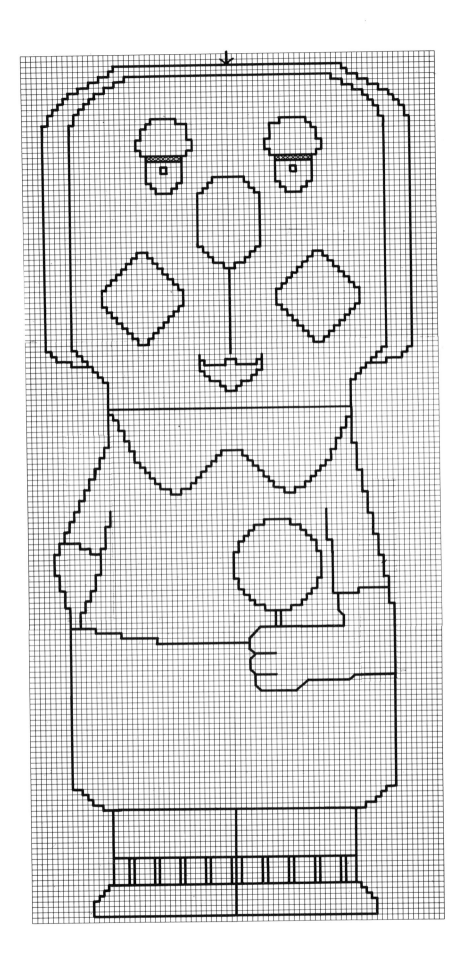

88

Lolita

STITCHES
Continental or Basketweave; Hair

YARN COLORS
Hair: *dark brown*
Skin: *beige*
Eyelids: *royal blue*
Eyeballs: *royal blue*
Eyes: *white*
Nose: *peach*
Cheeks: *peach*
Lip line: *peach*
Mouth: *red*
Collar: *white*
Sleeves: *maroon with brown arm outline*
Blouse: *shocking pink*
Lollipop: *red with brown stick*
Hands: *beige with pink outline*
Skirt: *lavender*
Legs: *beige with brown divider*
Socks: *orange and green with brown divider*
Shoes: *black with brown divider*

90

Ms. Pea

STITCHES
Continental or Basketweave; Hair

YARN COLORS
Hair: *gold*
Skin: *flesh*
Eyelids: *light green*
Eyelashes: *brown*
Eyeballs: *blue*
Eyes: *white*
Eye outline: *dark blue*
Nose: *shocking pink*
Mouth: *red*
Chin line and rouge: *lavender*
Bathing suit: *medium blue*
Banner: *green with light green letters*
Legs: *flesh with tan divider*
Shoes: *brown with tan divider*

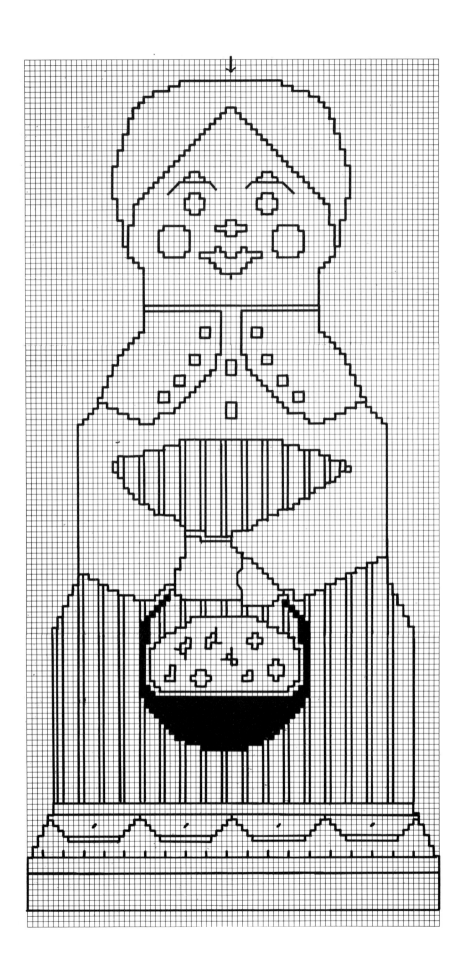

Bridgett

STITCH
Continental or Basketweave

YARN COLORS
Hair: *black*
Eyebrows: *black*
Eyeballs: *royal blue*
Nose: *pink*
Rouge: *light red*
Mouth: *red*
Skin: *white*
Collar: *gray with blue border and blue buttons*
Buttons: *white*
Shawl: *red*
Dress: *royal blue and orange vertical stripes*
Mitts: *light gold with black outline*
Basket: *dark gray*
Flowers: *red on green background*
Dress border: *royal blue outline on white background with orange dots*
End border: *red*

93

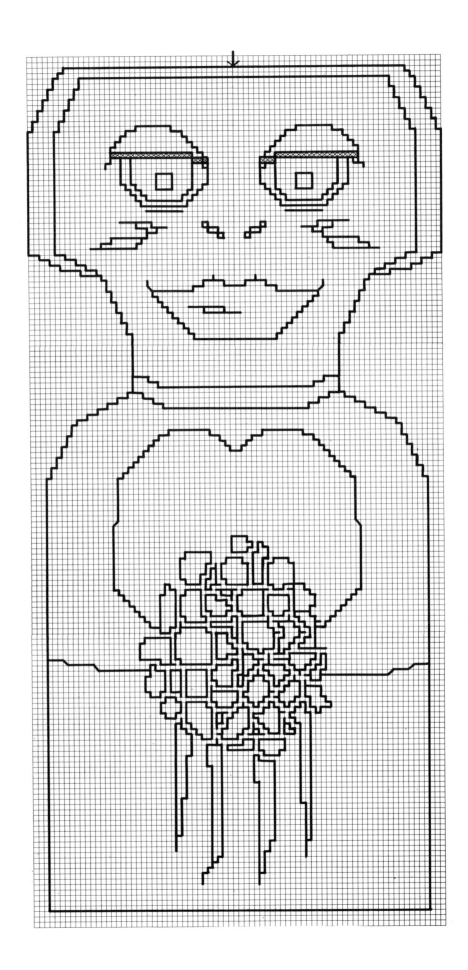

Carol

STITCHES
Continental or Basketweave; Hair

YARN COLORS
Hair: *light brown*
Skin: *pink*
Eyelids: *maroon*
Eyelashes: *black*
Eyes: *light brown*
Under eyes: *black*
Cheeks: *dark pink*
Nose: *dark pink*
Mouth: *red with pink flare*
Choker: *dark pink*
Dress: *dark pink with black outline*
Flowers: *any bright colors*
Ribbons: *light gray*

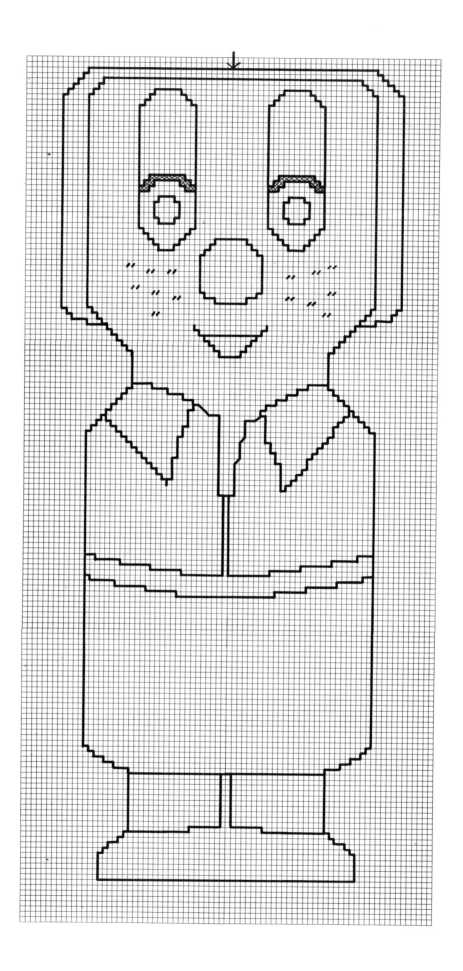

School Marm

STITCHES
Continental or Basketweave; Hair

YARN COLORS
Hair: *yellow*
Skin: *pink*
Eyelids: *silver gray*
Eyelashes: *brown*
Eyeballs: *brown*
Eyes: *white*
Nose: *orange*
Freckles: *orange*
Mouth: *red*
Collar: *white*
Shirt: *royal blue with gold outline*
Belt: *gold*
Skirt: *lemon yellow*
Stockings: *vertical stripes of any colors*
Shoes: *black*

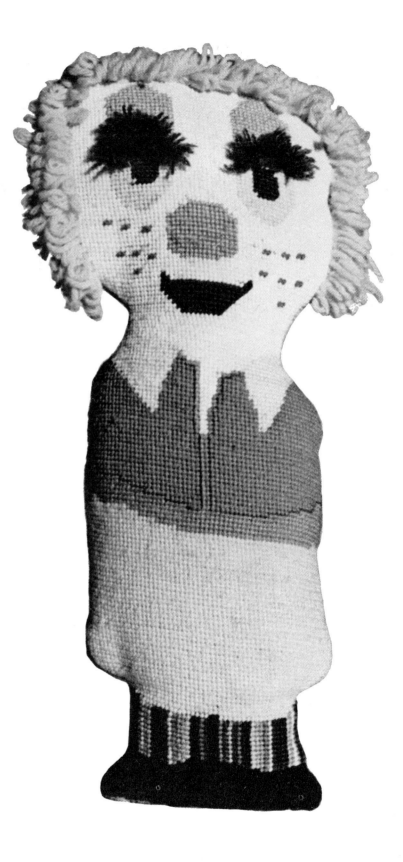

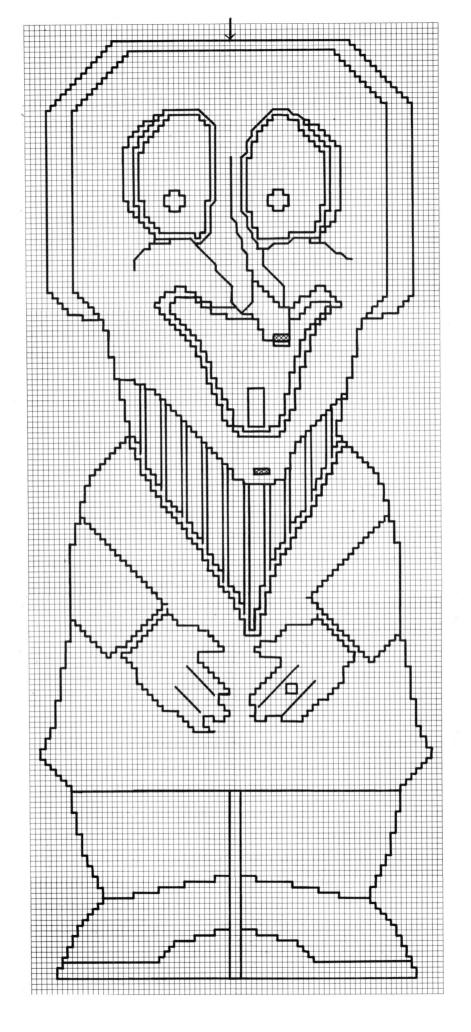

Wella Witch

STITCHES
Continental or Basketweave; Hair;
  sleeves in Brick; pants in Brick

YARN COLORS
Hair: *black*
Eyes: *pale yellow*
Eyeballs: *black*
Eye outline: *dark green*
Nose outline: *dark green*
Skin: *kelly green*
Lips: *light blue*
Inside mouth: *pink*
Tooth: *white*
Nose and chin hair: *black*
Sweater: *maroon and orange vertical
  stripes*
Arm outline: *brown*
Jacket: *black*
Hands: *kelly green with dark green
  outline*
Ring: *yellow*
Pants: *pink and yellow with brown
  divider*
Shoes: *orange with brown heels*

Nurse

STITCHES
Continental or Basketweave; Hair

YARN COLORS
Hair: *light gold*
Skin: *pink*
Eyelids: *royal blue*
Eyelashes: *royal blue*
Eyeballs: *royal blue*
Nose: *deep pink*
Mouth: *red*
Dress: *white with black outlines*
Thermometer: *red with black outline*
Cross: *red*
Hands: *pink with dark pink outline*
Hotwater bottle: *maroon*
Top of bottle: *black*
Cap, stockings, and shoes: *white*

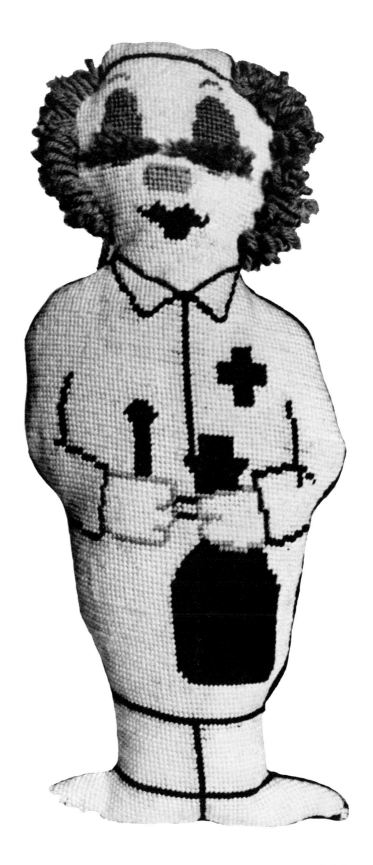

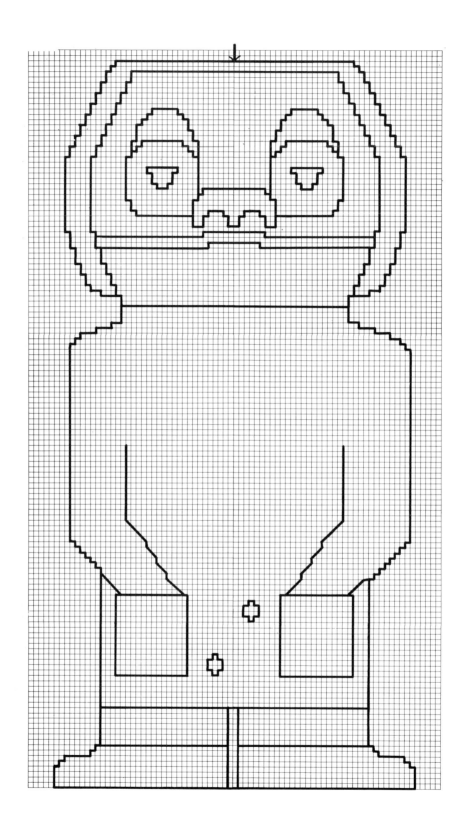

The Hippie

STITCHES
Continental or Basketweave; Hair; coat
 in Brick

YARN COLORS
Hair and beard: *dark brown*
Skin: *flesh*
Eyelids: *dark blue*
Eyes: *silver gray*
Eyeballs: *brown*
Nose: *medium pink*
Coat: *bright orange with black outlines*
Buttons: *black*
Pants: *bright yellow with black divider*
Shoes: *dark brown with black divider*

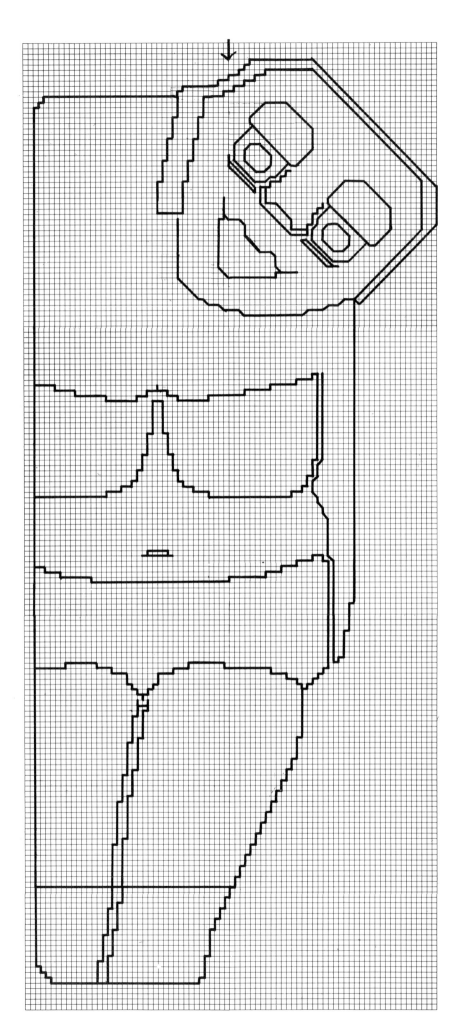

Sweet Lorraine

STITCHES
Continental or Basketweave; Hair

YARN COLORS
Hair: *lemon yellow*
Eyelids: *purple*
Eyes: *white*
Eyeballs: *pale blue*
Nose: *medium pink*
Lips: *red*
Chin and arm outline: *orange*
Bathing suit: *maroon*
Shoes: *red with brown divider*
Leg divider: *orange*
Skin: *flesh*

Emmett

STITCHES
Continental or Basketweave; Hair

YARN COLORS
Hair: *orange*
Skin: *white*
Eyelids: *dark gray*
Eyeballs: *dark blue*
Nose: *red*
Mouth: *red*
Rouge: *red and white*
Collar: *yellow with purple circles*
Coat: *shocking pink*
Buttons: *medium gray*
Shirt: *apple green*
Pocket and pants outline: *gray*
Handkerchief: *purple*
Arm outline: *black*
Shoes: *black*
Belt: *dark blue*
Pants: *lavender and purple checks*

4

From Canvas to Pillow

Your canvas should now be finished. In the spirit of this book we hope that you really enjoyed working on your doll and, perhaps, had a laugh or two when stitching the mouth or eyes. We have discovered that the big laugh usually comes after the hair has been finished and we stand back to look at our work. For some reason these little people always bring a smile.

Once you have admired your work, it is time to think about turning the canvas into a pillow. If you hate to sew, don't even bother about this last step. Look up a pillowmaker in the phone book and let him do the hard work. As you can probably tell from that last remark, although we love to needlepoint, pillowmaking is not our favorite pastime. We have learned to endure this step simply because we cannot afford to pay someone else the $15 to $20 to finish a pillow. If you really love this hobby, the cost can be considerable. Therefore, we do it ourselves, remembering with every stitch how much money we are saving.

Before beginning the pillow, you must first block the canvas, thereby restoring the canvas to its original shape. This is undoubtedly the most important step in completing the doll. If the blocking is not done correctly, all your hard work will be for nothing. The doll will look sloppy and unprofessional. As we mentioned earlier, the needlepoint stitch produces a diagonal tension that tends to pull the mesh. The amount of distortion depends on the type of stitch used. Remember, you will have a lot less blocking work if you use the Basketweave instead of the Continental stitch.

Whichever stitch is used, however, blocking is usually required. The first step is to wet your finished canvas completely. Fill a basin with lukewarm water and let the canvas soak for a minute or two. Sometimes while you have been working on the design, certain areas will become soiled. In our case, we both own dogs, and they have a fondness for placing their paws on the canvas. Today's air pollution also can make your yarn dirty. This especially holds true for city dwellers who live in high levels of smog. There really is no way to keep your needlepoint clean while working on it. There is just too much dirt around. Anyway, now is the time to clean the yarn. Add a little Woolite to cold water so it will not shrink. A washing will clean the design and leave the yarn looking fresh and bright.

You can now understand why we urge you to take every precaution when choosing a marker to draw the design. If it is not completely waterproof, it will probably run during this soaking period.

Before you begin to block, partially dry the canvas by placing it between two towels. Roll the towels up and squeeze. Do not wring! We recommend doing this on the floor. You can kneel on the rolled towels and exert more pressure. This step should absorb most of the water from the yarn and decrease the drying time considerably.

You will need a blocking board now. It is best to get a piece about two by four feet; this size will accommodate just about any canvas you will ever want to needlepoint for a pillow. We use a drawing board, available at most art stores. This board is about an inch thick, but hollow inside, which makes tacking the canvas to the board a lot easier. You can, however, use just about anything around the house. Some people pull out the old cardtable.

To make this whole process less work, remember to cut the selvage about every three inches. The selvage, by the way, is that very closely woven mesh on the edge of the canvas. Cutting through the selvage will make it easier for you to pull the canvas back into shape.

Now cover the board with a piece of paper. Using the waterproof marker, draw a vertical line down the center of the paper, and then draw a horizontal line at a right angle across the vertical. These lines will be your guides in pulling the canvas back to its original shape.

You may, of course, add additional lines. The more points of reference you have on the paper, the easier your job will be.

You are now ready to begin pinning the canvas to the board. Many professionals suggest using rustproof tacks or pushpins for the job. Pushpins are much easier to use with their built-in handles.

Lay the canvas face down on the paper, tuck all hair in, then line up one side with a vertical line. Pin the edge of the canvas down securely, spacing the pushpins about every inch or so. You will discover that the tape you used to prevent the edges from fraying also becomes a convenient place to stick the pins. Once you have secured the side, move to another side perpendicular to the first. Again pull the canvas secure so that this side lines up with a horizontal line. This may be difficult for the beginner; it takes quite a bit of effort to pull the mesh back into shape. It is best to work from the corner nearest the first side pinned down. You should be looking for two things. First, the corners must come to right angles. Second, all the canvas strands should end up just as straight as you can possibly make them. This will take time and patience, but believe us, it is worth the effort.

After you have pinned down two sides, work on the remaining sides. This is where real muscle must be applied; the canvas will resist your pulls and tugs. We should give another helpful hint that we have learned. After you have wet the canvas, you will notice that the mesh becomes slippery to handle, owing to the sizing applied by the manufacturer. Often, when pulling, the canvas will slip right out of your fingers and drive you crazy. To get around this problem you might want to wear a pair of thin cotton gloves. You will be able to grasp the edge much better. The pulling and pinning operation usually takes about fifteen minutes to half an hour to complete. So take your time and do it right.

Once you have completed the blocking, set the board aside and let it dry thoroughly. At this point you may want to spray the wet canvas with sizing. We usually put the board in a closet and forget about it for a day or so. Unless the canvas is exceptionally large, and none for the Pillow People is, it will dry overnight.

Now you are ready to start making the pillow. Take the blocking board from the closet and unpin the canvas. This is the time to find out whether your efforts have succeeded or failed. If the canvas is still out of shape, you really ought to reblock. This may bring tears to your eyes, but facts are facts. If the blocking is not correct, your doll will always stand just a little crooked. Of course, a lot of people may decide that a doll on the slant is better than the agony of reblocking. That is up to you and your doll.

The fabric you choose for the backing is an important part of the overall look of the doll. We have worked with corduroy, velvetine, crushed velvet, and most of the knitted fabrics. Each has its own effect, such as the corduroys that add an extra tactile as well as visual sensation. We have found the knitted fabrics seem to work best as backing, especially the ones that will stretch just a little. This give makes your stuffing task easier, and the doll becomes shapelier. When selecting your fabric give a lot of thought to color. Try to coordinate the backing with one of the dominant colors in the design. This will not only be more pleasing to the eye, but will add more fun to the doll as well. There is the other school of thought that maintains the back should be black so as not to detract from the front. The final decision is up to you.

It is time to bring out the sewing machine once you have selected the backing. We do not recommend trying to hand-sew the pillow, although it probably can be done. The stitch binding the canvas and backing should be very small, producing a strong seam.

Cut the fabric about two inches larger than the doll and lay the canvas on top of the fabric. The two front sides should be facing each other, because the pillow will be made inside out. Now pin the canvas and fabric together, making sure that all the hair is tucked in toward the middle of the head. If you neglect to do this, some of the hair may be stitched inside the pillow and lost forever. The shorter the hair, the more difficult it will be to control the problem. When we have a particularly hard time making sure all the hair gets in and not out, we tape the hair down to the face. That is a simple step, but it guarantees that all your work will be seen.

Once you have pinned the canvas and fabric together, machine-sew three sides together, leaving the bottom open. It's best to work slowly and guide the machine as close as possible to the border of your needlepoint work. You will probably have to give up two stitches in the process; sewing in any more than this is a waste of material and leaves you with less needlepoint exposed.

The neck area can sometimes present a problem when it is time to stuff the pillow. Try not to make any abrupt changes in stitch direction when sewing this area. The neck should be a curve from the shoulders to the head and not an angle. The curve looks better and will not pinch the fabric.

After the sides are sewn together, remove all the pins and trim off the excess canvas and fabric. Try to trim close to the machine stitch, especially in the corner areas; this makes it easier to stuff. Now it is time to turn the doll right-side-out. Reach in through the bottom, grab the head or hair, and pull it through the opening. When it is turned out, take your first look at the almost complete doll.

Before stuffing the pillow, make sure all the edges are pushed out as far as possible. You might want to press the seam with a steam iron. The best material for stuffing is polyester acrylic fiber. This is probably the least expensive and is available in bags at most five-and-ten-cent stores. It is dense enough to keep the pillow in shape and soft enough to be very comfortable.

Do not overstuff your doll. There is nothing worse than picking up a doll that feels like a rock. Remember, you are making a pillow that should have plenty of give so it will be a joy to lean against or cuddle. When stuffing the neck area, use one hunk of fiber to fill from the head to the chest. We've learned that if this area is filled with smaller pieces, the neck tends to wobble because of inadequate support. Don't let any of the little corners go without stuffing. You don't want to overstuff, but you should at least fill in all the areas.

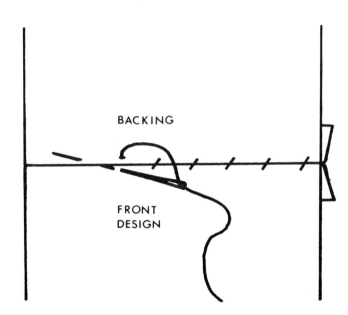

BACKING

FRONT
DESIGN

The doll is now ready for the final seam at the bottom. Here the canvas and the fabric will be sewn together using the blindstitch. And that's exactly what it is. When done properly the thread will not show because the fabric itself will tend partially to cover the stitch. Again try to sew the seam so that it will cover only two needlepoint stitches along the bottom. As you sew across, keep adding little bits of stuffing to fill in the feet.

Guess what? You are finished! Now we suggest you pick up the new doll, place her on the sofa, walk across the room, and take your first good look at the little devil. We are sure you will be just as amused at what you see as we have been. You now have a new, very quiet member of the family.

5

The Pillow People

As we mentioned at the beginning, we first started designing and making our dolls as gifts for our friends. We now would like to thank everyone who cheerfully returned their dolls to us so we could assemble them for this book. We must admit that we have had quite a time with all the little people around. When not away being photographed or sketched, all the dolls were kept on the sofa and chairs in our office. What a sight it was! Forty little creatures just standing around and saying nothing. At times the office began to look like the waiting room in a train station. During business meetings they all seemed to become silent partners patiently awaiting the outcome of a big business deal.

What we learned from having the gang around is that the more you make, the more fun the Pillow People become. They're like peanuts; once you have one, you want more. A grouping of three or four standing next to a fireplace can be an amusing sight.

We named all the dolls. We couldn't help it, because they are like children. If you are going to talk about them, you have to call them something. But our names don't necessarily have to be your names. We are sure that you can dream up much more suitable names for them. Everyone has an Uncle Harry or Aunt Viola willing to share their name.

We have learned one important thing from our friends about the little people. They should not be thought of as toys. Children who have received them as gifts do not think of the dolls this way. On the contrary, most of the kids handle them with a certain amount of respect. The doll is more a friend than a plaything. A godchild, Cara Burnham, even gave her doll, Wella Witch, a haircut!

As friends, the Pillow People should be found all over the house. The living room, of course, is the natural place to put one of the dolls. As we said, they really do look funny sitting at the end of a sofa. But use your imagination. Why not try the kitchen? What could be a better room for Bertha Baker, our favorite cook? Most of the dolls are perfect additions to any child's room. Plus, they are great companions for any youngster. Wella Witch, Emmett, and Baby Doll are a few of the children's favorites.

When we began making our dolls, all our friends wanted one of their own. Not knowing it, we had created a marvelous gift idea. This made the usual torture of selecting presents a lot easier. At Christmas the kids all received their favorite dolls. The Pillow People also simplified birthdays. Dad's green thumb was rewarded with The Gardener, a nephew active in high school athletics got Muscles Morris, an the old family physician naturally received Doc. If you are good at needlepointing letters, you might want to personalize one of the dolls by adding a name or initials somewhere on the clothing. Our Ms. Pea beauty contestant is a perfect example. All you have to do is ignore our lettering and substitute your own for a very personalized gift.

We have found that the Pillow People are welcomed far more than something bought at the local department store. The dolls are handmade, and all the time and effort that is put into their creation is appreciated. The very nature of handicrafts involves the personal satisfaction one derives from making something out of nothing. The finished work, whether it is a doll or a painting, has built into it lots of love, care, and attention. When it is given as a gift, all this emotion goes with it. You will see. All you have to do is watch the reaction when the wrapping paper is removed. All those hours of stitching will suddenly become worth much more to you because they were spent making something meaningful for someone else. What could be a more rewarding pastime?

2512   1